I am always with you

> *Thy hand is on my head and my heart is on thy feet*
> *Thus have we been interlocked, body into body, self into self*
> *It is mine to serve and thine to favour*
>
> Tukaram

 Om Sai Shri Sai Jai Jai Sai

I am always with you

Lorraine Walshe-Ryan

Marketed in Shirdi by:
Anand Novelties
Near Hanuman Temple, Shirdi-423 109
Telephone: (02423) 255543

STERLING PAPERBACKS
An imprint of
Sterling Publishers (P) Ltd.
A-59, Okhla Industrial Area, Phase-II,
New Delhi-110020.
Tel: 26387070, 26386209; Fax: 91-11-26383788
E-mail: sterlingpublishers@airtelmail.in
ghai@nde.vsnl.net.in
www.sterlingpublishers.com

I Am Always With You
© 2006, Lorraine Walshe-Ryan
ISBN 978-81-207-3192-9
Reprint 2008, 2010, 2014

All rights are reserved.
No part of this publication may be reproduced, stored in a retrieval system or transmitted, in any form or by any means, mechanical, photocopying, recording or otherwise, without prior written permission of the original publisher.

Printed and Published by Sterling Publishers Pvt. Ltd.,
New Delhi-110 020.

Dedicated to my Hazrat Shirdi Sai Baba—my Everything to Sathya Sai Baba (Swami) for His Divine help and grace in bringing me to my beloved Shirdi Sai Baba's Feet, to Jesus and all the heavenly beings in my puja room and to my darling child Lisa, my loving family and dear friends.

Do not think of me and weep
I am with you still, I do not sleep
I am a thousand winds that blow
I am the diamond glints on snow
I am the sunlight on refined grain
I am the gentle autumn rain
When you awaken in the morning hush
I am the swift, uplifting rush of quiet birds in circled flight
I am the soft stars that shine at night
Do not think of me and cry
I am with you still – I DID NOT DIE

Anonymous

And So He is, Ever With Me

Lorraine Walshe-Ryan
2004

Contents

Forewords	viii-ix
Preface	xi
Acknowledgements	xii

Year

1993	1
1995	2
1996	4
1997	6
1998	17
1999	39
2000	65
2001	86
2002	111
2003	132
2004	158
Epilogue	179

Foreword

I have known Lorraine since 1997 and have witnessed the incredible effect her experiences have had on her. She is a truly unique person in that she lives what she believes and moreover is a genuine and caring individual. I cannot speak highly enough about her.

Lorraine, I am very excited for you, as I can see this is truly a labour of your love for Sai. You have done a great job in creating this compilation of your experiences and putting them onto paper for others to enjoy and understand that once you surrender to His Will, He will take care of you.

Radhakrishnan Kottieth Pullambil

Foreword

I have great pleasure in writing this Foreword at the request of the author - one steeped in spirituality. Reflecting on the Lorraine Ryan I know, I am reminded of the words in the hymn Amazing Grace – 'I once was lost but now am found; was blind but now I see'.

The spark of divinity exists in the core of our being. A time comes during our sojourn on earth when we experience a thirst, a yearning to find out who we truly are. When this yearning becomes intense, tinged with true faith and devotion, an enlightened soul crosses our path. This great soul has in His mission, a task to lead those who are ready, to the Light. Despite the many trials in the author's life, she was blessed with a steady stream of such great souls to lead her back onto the spiritual path. This book is an interesting compilation of her life's story, sprinkled with spiritual thoughts and actions, providing readers with a source of inspiration and encouragement to respond to the challenge at hand.

I Am Always With You traces Lorraine's life's journey on earth from childhood with Jesus as her friend and companion to Sathya Sai Baba and finally finding her true Divine Master, Shirdi Sai. It records how surrendering to Shirdi Sai has enabled her to experience His love each day making life that much more bearable. In fact it helps her look forward to the next day. In the time I have known Lorraine, she has always struck me as one who is sincere in her quest – to quench her spiritual thirst.

I commend Lorraine on her 'labour of love' and pray her sincere efforts will benefit many a reader in their hour of need. God bless.

Sydney, Krishnan Nair
Australia.

Om Shri Ganapathy Namaha

Preface

Things happened very rapidly. I vaguely remember hearing about Swami (Sathya Sai Baba) as a child or a teenager, but being indoctrinated into the Catholic faith, no other religion was taught or spoken of in our household, even though we lived between Hindus and Muslims in Calcutta, India, where I was born and raised. We were Catholics and only knew of 'Sweet Jesus'; 'thank Heavens', my Sweet Jesus is still with me.

In writing this book, it is solely 'The Doer' Shirdi Sai along with Sathya Sai and Jesus, with whose inspiration and guidance, it has been completed after nine years. During these years I have seen the changes in my life. I who loved to smoke, drink and party, now prefers to stay home, pray, be silent, whenever the opportunity arises help the needy, feed the poor, be compassionate and helpful, and most of all, to make people laugh or at least put a smile on their face. Writing this book has been possible only because of Baba's Grace, who along with Sathya Sai and Jesus have been 'the Doers' and me merely following their instructions.

I pray this book with Baba's grace, be a reality to those who believe in the Divinity within Them. I am That, for He is always with you (and me).

April 2006   Lorraine Walshe-Ryan

Acknowledgements

Many many thanks to the three Gurus (i.e., Shirdi Sai, Sathya Sai and Jesus Sai*), my family and the many wonderful Sai friends I have encountered in this journey, to Henry L. who has helped me on countless occasions with the photocopying, printing and saving my data for me.

Sincere thanks to all.

* Readers please note that reference is made to Sathya Sai Baba as Swami and Shirdi Sai Baba as Baba.

1993

I was in a state of forlornness due to family matters. I was lying, sunbaking in the backyard of our home, looking at a very beautiful blue sky, talking to God to help our child find a job. A cloud started to form into the distinct shape of India and I was mesmerised by its clarity and shape. The phone rang, it was my daughter telling me she had been employed. Thank You God.

My first real information on Sathya Sai Baba (Swami) was when I noticed a nurse (Australian) at the hospital we worked at (I now live in Australia), wearing the *Om* sign and intensely reading a book on Swami, (I noticed the bushy hair on the cover and the glaring *Orange Dress*). I could not contain my curiosity and questioned her about the book. She started relating to me all about her visits to India to see Swami, about vibhuti, her shrine at home and asked me if I would like to read about Swami, thereby lending me a book, *The Holy Man and the Psychiatrist*, and a few other books. I read them all and though my curiosity was aroused, I merely passed it off as another cult figure (apologies Swami). Things then began to occur very subtlely for me. The Gurus were arriving!

A few months later, I began to read a lot of books on Swami, but due to my utter despair of an impending divorce, along with thoughts of 'suicide' I decided to visit a herbalist/naturopath. On entering the clinic in Kingsford, Sydney, I noticed a little picture of this Swami (the guru I had been reading about) and in going into the consulting room, a large calendar with Swami's picture smiling down at me. I forgot my illness, why I was there initially, and wanted to speak only of this Swami. David, the naturopath explained to me about his family's devotion to this Holy Man in India, about the bhajans (did not know prior to this what a bhajan was), etc. He invited me to participate in same, but I declined. This was the start of my divine journey, may it be forevermore, although over the last eighteen months after this, there was no other contact, i.e., reading about or seeing Swami.

1995

April

I decided to go to Cairns for a holiday to see my friend Dianne (also referred as Di)and her family whom I had not seen for a few years, after they had left Sydney and also to recover from my traumatic divorce. Ever caring as always, Di was concerned about my mental state and health and decided to take me to see her herbalist in Cairns.

On entering Ruth's clinic, I was 'knocked out' by a picture of Swami in the foyer, and I made a comment in a jocular manner to the picture – 'hey, are You following me? I have not seen You in a few months'. Di asked me who The Man in the Orange Robe was, (mind you Ruth was her friend and naturopath, Di visited practically every week, and never commented before on This orange robed figure) and asked me if I knew Him. I replied, 'Of course not, I have merely read a book or two about Him'. After being introduced to Ruth and having my session with her, we briefly talked of Swami. It was a Thursday and Ruth invited us to attend bhajans at her home. Di and I were both baffled by the word bhajans, but nonetheless we accepted.

At Ruth's home that evening it was awesome—we had entered into *another era*. The lights were dim, there were people sitting on the floor in front of a rather large and imposing picture of Swami. There was an altar decorated with flowers, incense and fruit, people were singing unfamiliar songs in an unfamiliar language, especially for Dinky Di. I was familiar with the Indian language, having been born and raised in India up to the age of 23, but not having practised the language in so many years. Now being an Australian citizen, it sounded quite beautiful. Di and I were amazed, amused, and just watched.

During the meditation, the lights were further dimmed, Di nudged me and asked me if I had seen what happened. I hadn't as my eyes were shut. She then whispered that she had seen the whole huge gold-framed picture of this Swami swing to one side and then back to its original position and the garland from the picture falling off. I was a bit upset as I had not actually seen this, but all the same baffled and skeptical as there was no wind, no fans, and being in a room with other people, no one else had noticed it except Di. Later that evening, Ruth explained that it was Swami making His presence felt. Di was happy, I was not, in fact, I was downright angry and disappointed having seen nothing.

After returning to Sydney I could not wait to hear more about this mysterious Swami. Di used to ring me often as she had started attending the bhajans on Thursdays, also kindly sending me pictures of Swami, and an old man called Shirdi Baba. I was confused enough with Swami and took not much notice of Shirdi Baba, except to notice He was a rather handsome Guru, but I was trying hard to get to know Swami through the books that I had read. Shirdi was at the bottom of the pile and not much attention was paid to Him at this time. I had rented a flat in Randwick and to supplement my income, I housed students. One of my Japanese students saw a picture of Swami in my home and commented that Swami was very famous in Japan, and apparently was on TV there for half an hour every day. I was a bit disappointed that He was not on Australian TV.

1996

Getting more involved with Swami, i.e., reading books and trying to get as much information on Swami, literally buying books from The Sai Centre, St. Ives and elsewhere, I just could not seem to read enough about Sathya Sai Baba. I am amazed how my eyesight held out. Life seemed to be very gradually changing.

With Swami's Grace, I gave up my rented accommodation in the expensive eastern suburbs of Sydney and mortgaged a small villa in the south-western suburbs. But by this time, I was beginning to become more aware of the old man mentioned earlier, Shirdi Sai Baba, who was filling my heart and mind with His thoughts. I had heard about Him in a conversation with friends at a unity bhajan which I had now begun to attend and bought the *Sai Satcharita* there and read it three times. Shirdi Sai was coming into my life in even a bigger way, but very slowly (saburi). I just loved the book and I was beginning to love this very humble, simple, beautiful Shirdi Baba, at the same time, being in awe of Swami but my heart and mind were heading in the direction of Shirdi Sai.

My fiftieth birthday was approaching and I had decided to go to Europe with my mother and sister. I asked Swami for His guidance and help as to whether I could afford the trip and to please give me a sign. The next morning on the way to work in the train, I noticed three words etched into the seat in front of me 'Travel Travel Travel'. My first answer and my first sign from Swami! *Koti koti pranaams Swami* (still don't know what Koti means, perhaps I hope Thanks).

We had a wonderful holiday around Europe, but the highlight for me was the Murano Glass factory in Italy. I had purchased a little vase and on removing my Visa card from my wallet to pay the account, the store attendant noticed a picture of Swami in my wallet. He said, 'Oh Sai Baba!' I was stunned that someone in Europe (no not my ego, just simplicity about the magnanimity of

Swami, I thought, at this stage, that He was only known in India [my ignorance] and a small portion of Australia) should know of Swami. I was told in no uncertain terms that most of Venice/Italy knew of Swami, loved Him and were followers, and at that particular time, He was in India . I was much pleased and impressed. I have since heard that the whole Viennese Orchestra was taken to India for Swami's birthday to play for Him.

I have always had a 'fear of flying', my sister Sharon being a bigger coward than me. Whenever we travelled overseas, we both had a few drinks and tranquillisers to keep us calm. During this trip to and around Europe and return, we experienced the most tranquil journey (with very minor turbulences for such a long journey). *Koti koti pranaams* Swami, it had to be You. I chanted '*Sai Sai*' all the way, every day and everywhere. We all returned home safely and happily, thank You Swami, note here dear readers, Shirdi Sai was not given much thought at this time. I was just getting to know Swami though.

During one of our shopping trips in London, I saw a few knick-knacks of Swami and the distinguished old Baba, Shirdi Sai, and I bought a few of these things, not from knowledge but as mere souvenirs. Then when I returned to Australia, Di and I were still having our discussions about Swami, when I was invited to participate in Swami's seventy-first birthday celebrations. Through my 'Book Club' I managed to get a phone number of a couple living in Raby who generously asked me to accompany them to the Birthday celebrations (23.11.96). This was my first experience of a Swami *throng* (crowd). Hundreds of Indians/others, all finely attired, were present. The hall was very crowded, the altar was beautifully decorated, especially at the *feet* (a novice here). There was a beautiful lotus made out of rice grains, also Swami's chair with His 'kerchief'. After bhajans that the children performed, a gentleman gave a speech. After the services, we were all given a brown paper bag with delicious Indian food, apples and packets of vibhuti, me being amazed and unfamiliar with all these 'goings-on'.

1997

I decided to resign from my job in Randwick as it was becoming very tiring to travel for four hours a day to work and back, and I was confident that with my experience, it would not take me that long to find another job. I had stopped working and it had been three weeks, during which I was getting fearful and was 'blabbering' endlessly with Swami, reading the Bible, Bhagavad Gita, *Satcharita* again, lighting incense, praying that Swami was listening, and hoping that He would give me the right job at the right time, but soon.

My First Dream

Two weeks ago I had a dream where I was talking to Swami, whose eyes were glowing green in colour. We were both looking at a book and He mentioned one of the men in the book being Gandhiji. I then looked up and saw Shirdi Baba walking towards us, but He didn't look very happy (I do call him my 'grumpy old man' with much affection). The dream ended here but I was unable to decipher it. The following night I dreamt about the number 1575 which adds up to nine, which is Baba's number. I had another dream of drinking water with which I had just washed somebody's feet. I don't know whose feet, but I was told it was dirty water. I retorted that it was okay, I didn't mind and that I would be all right. This was the end of the dream.

March

On 9 March, I was invited to bhajans in Raby, Sydney at St. Andrew's Scout Hall with Kala and Henry Subramaniam a very kind couple living in Leumeah. There was about sixteen of us at that first bhajan. The men swept the hall and the ladies decorated the altar. I watched, listened to them and clapped but did not sing, as I didn't know the lyrics or the language. A very kindly gentleman then asked me to read a passage, from a tiny book, which I gladly did, but failed to turn on the microphone (didn't know how, to be honest and was feeling nervous). The ladies had the most beautiful voices. The kind gentleman was our co-ordinator named Radha. After meditation, a lad named Rohit asked me to sing an English bhajan. I declined as I was too shy. During the study circle, Rohit again asked me to sing, so I then explained to all about my throat cancer in the past, having no saliva and breath control, therefore being unable to sing at all, although I could read. After bhajans, I was approached by Radha who took my phone number and told me he would give me some sacred water to drink. I looked forward to this and asked all to pray to Swami for me, as I was, at that time, having trouble with the throat again, and also to pray to Swami that I would find a job again. I was reading *My Baba and I* by Dr John Hislop, a blessed man, who had received so much from His Grace. Oh Swami, what about me? Is it too early to ask yet?

****

Radha rang tonight; such a loving devotee, he spoke with such reverence for about forty minutes on Swami. I admired his dedication. He was bringing me the lingam water on Sunday and would return some time next week to discuss our Beloved Swami. He loved to talk of Swami and I loved to listen.

****

In my dream I saw a woman sitting in a warm, sunny room. I suddenly got the most beautiful and strong aroma of roses and I said aloud – 'Swami are You here?' There was a strong breeze, my hair all stood up and I began levitating, my head almost touching the roof. I chanted Swami's name all the while. When I got down, I could see a man pointing to me and saying – 'She believes in something called Sai'. I then saw three boys dressed in long orange robes, with Swami's hairstyle (a young version of Swami). They smiled at me and gave me some food, I smiled back at them. This was the end of my dream.

****

I had a very pleasant visit from Radhakrishnan. He brought me the sacred lingam water which I shall treasure, the lingam picture of Swami and a book titled *Living Divinity*. Here was a very humble and pleasant human being and a loving devotee. I could not put down the book he gave me, as a result of which I had sore eyes.

My First Leela (23 March)

The nurse who first introduced me to Swami, at that time also gave me a phial of amrit. A mere drop. This has travelled from house to house with me and I have never actually paid any attention to it, not knowing what amrit was. Last week though, while I was clearing out the cupboards, I discovered this dirty almost empty phial, realising it to be the amrit given to me. I quickly cleaned it and placed it on the altar. It is now about halfway up the phial, clean, clear and sweet.

April

My First Experience at Making Garlands for Swami

I was invited to Kala's home and I watched and tried to help the ladies thread flowers and make garlands. This was quite an experience. I wished to do anything for Swami even if I didn't do a good job except prick my finger. I attended bhajan sessions, was moved to tears by the beautiful voice of Savita, who sings like a nightingale. Radha lent me a book *A Journey to Love*. I read the book in one day, it is simply written and very enjoyable. In such a short space of time, the author has received so many interviews, leelas and materialisations from Swami. I would be grateful for but one.

My Two Mini Leelas

On a few occasions on reading Swami's books, I have been getting the strong and sweet smell of vibhuti. Before going to an interview today (15 April) I asked Swami, 'Please give me an OK that things will go OK (the humour behind the work OK). On entering the place I noticed one of the doctor's names being cheOK I had a giggle. I got a temporary job. I thanked Swami and my sister Cheryl.

****

I saw myself around a lot of Indian men and women, shouting *Sai Ram* and *Om*. My dream ended here. I thought that perhaps one day I will be there with them doing just that.

29 April

My mother spent the weekend with me, we ended up having a 'heated debate' on Swami. She commented on Swami's many pictures in the home and none of the family. She was also concerned about my not taking interest in any family affairs/ matters, I appeared detached and uncaring. The weekend did not go very well, my mother clearly indicating that she was rather perturbed about me worshipping a Man.. *Om Sai Ram*

May

On the way to the city by train to meet a friend from South Africa, I was thinking of Shirdi Baba for some reason, and not Swami, and vaguely asking for a sign that it would be a pleasant day and not one of bickering between my mother and myself, as we were really battling about Swami. I looked at the window-pane of the train and saw clearly etched in the glass, the sign *Om*. I smiled.

The Divine Light

I was doing my aarti puja when the face of Swami started moving and changing like a 'hologram'. It kept on for a while. I felt blessed, at last. I smiled back at Swami calmly. I told Kala.

It happened again, the face seemed to be fading and turning yellow. At one stage the *Om* sign on Shirdi Baba's hand disappeared and a yellow light was seen. He even moved His lips. What is all this? I am not familiar with events of the *Divine* kind. I verbalised my *Yellow Episode* during the bhajan sessions held on Sunday. I was also very gregarious. We all had wonderful leelas to narrate on Swami, especially Vandana, whom Swami had blessed as she is now pregnant with her first child (and yes it was a beautiful bonny boy).

At home it happened again. I was doing the afternoon aarti, the pictures kept fading, this time mostly Shirdi Baba. The face changed. A light was shining on it and Baba's beard looked almost human. I was in awe.

June

After a week of weeping for darshan, it happened today. At aarti in my prayer room at home, Swami's face faded and came in forms of a young man. I smiled and was in bliss. I also am 'very happy'.

What a trickster is Swami. Before going to bhajans I divided the roses bought, in two bunches, one for the home altar and one for bhajans, three in the puja room and five for bhajans. After a long discussion on Swami, Rita a lady from our bhajan group handed me back an empty vase—there was not a single rose or petal, not even a flower from the altar. I had a good laugh as I wanted to take the roses back home for the puja room, but Swami made sure it was distributed and shared between all. *Share*, again nothing belongs to us; not my will but His persisted. I wanted to take all the flowers home again, but He showed me how to share.

Strange Dreams
In a dream early this morning, I saw Swami give a japamala to someone, a female, and she did not want it. I grabbed it saying, 'I'll have it'. Swami told me to take it but *not to tell anyone that He* had materialised. In real life, Sathya Sai Baba materialises with His hands, vibhuti, sometimes jewellery and japamalas for the many groups who are granted interviews by Sathya Sai Baba, in Puttaparthi, South India. The dream came to an end.

****

I had two dreams. First I saw Swami playing with some children and He looked at me straight in the eye, *very angry*. Swami sort of stared right through me. I knelt in front of Swami saying 'I love You Swami very much'. Lisa was with me and I said to her 'That's Sai Baba'. Swami then began to change His orange robe into a silver robe. The dream ended. On writing this I realise the dream. I made a comment to someone at work yesterday that I didn't tolerate children well. Thank You Swami, please keep reminding me to accept all. Lisa is my only child, I do tolerate her well though.

****

In another dream, I saw Mum, Lisa and me in a temple. There were various statues around and we decided to partake of the prasad offered. Mum was hacking away at a piece of food. I got upset with her and told her the food was sacred. I enjoyed the food very much, (fish in a leaf). This was the end of my dream. During bhajans, today, John gave me a tin with some vibhuti in it. I was very thankful.

****

July

The Lost Scarf
Thursday after work at Camden (and an awful blustery cold day), I walked home with my warm beautiful scarf I had bought in Ireland, trailing on my arm. At about 7 p.m. I felt that I had lost something,

and my senses were right, the scarf. I got into a state of utter despair (attachment to materialism) and pain with much sobbing. I loved the scarf so much because it was a sentimental item I had bought in Ireland, a place I became very endeared to, my father's family having originally come from Ireland. After much discussion and anger with Swami, I fell into a restless sleep. This morning, before I left for work, I again had an irate conversation, with Swami and reluctantly left for work. Just as I passed Tim's Garden Centre, I saw a flutter ahead of me. My scarf was hanging on a post. I ran for it with much joy and thankfulness in my heart. I was amazed that it had been there overnight, and no one had taken it, neither was it blown away by the cold winter wind.

Dreams

In my dream, I saw myself very frightened. I was either intending to go home or to work, but I was very scared. Mum was with me and I kept repeating, 'Swami is coming, Swami is coming and I am very scared to go alone'. Mum seemed to be angry herself and challenged me about Swami. I then saw us stand beside a stall of stale-looking food, the food started moving, and it all began to look fresh and healthy. I looked up at the sky and there was a very youthful Swami, smiling down at us. Mum looked up too but could not see Swami, Lisa was also with us and she saw Swami too. Then Swami came back to earth, put a robe around Himself and was approaching us. I was scared, elated, tearful, emotional, etc. When Swami was in front of me He put out His hand for me to touch it and also said something, which I never heard, but on looking at the figure again it was very dark, wizened, and more like Shirdi Baba. I awoke. I must state here that my most beloved Shirdi Baba is definitely not dark or wizened. This brought me to the end of the dream and I awoke.

****

On going back to sleep (4.30 a.m.), I had another dream. I saw a puja about to be performed, with many ladies in attendance. I tried to get involved and was handing Rita a few holy items when they fell out of my hands, the crucifix was broken and I became very distressed. But Rita picked them up and seemed to have fixed them and assured me not to worry, it would be okay. The dream ended here.

****

I got the saddest call from Kala. Satish was killed (Savita's brother) in a car accident. How can uttered words or thoughts describe the sadness of life? I could not sleep and when I did, I dreamt of Swami materialising Himself, but I was again afraid. I then saw myself trying to buy a miniscule statue of Our Lady. This was the end of the dream. May your soul be happy and at peace, Satish, darling boy.

****

During the noon aarti, the hologram appeared. The colour of Swami's face changed to white as well as the youthfulness of His appearance. Is this my imagination? I am doubting myself *not* Swami. What is this I see? It happened early this morning. I was meditating in the lounge room, and was speaking with Swami of all my sadness, when the *blue* light started shining through from the picture. I was elated. I know Swami is with me. This happened for about fifteen minutes and I looked at the other picture just to make sure my eyes were not playing tricks with me. It happened with this picture too. The light was radiating a blue aura, and Swami's face was covered by it. The appearance of Swami's face changed briefly and He was a youth again. I told Henry and Kala (Sai devotees, from our bhajan group). They feel Swami is here, so do I.

August

In my dream, I saw a person dressed in orange with hair all cut off. I cried, 'Swami You have cut off all Your hair', but on looking at the person again it was *not* Swami. I then started shouting to the crowd nearby, particularly my addressing mother, 'Gather together, Swami is going to perform a miracle'. I then looked up to see a Swastika on fire. The dream ended here.

****

During noon aarti, the face of Swami and Shirdi Baba changed, a yellow aura was seen, and the eyes moved. I asked Baba and I received permission from Baba for writing a book aptly titled *My Clown Prince*. I was doubting all the 'appearances and colours' of Swami and Shirdi Baba and on doing aarti this morning, I looked at Shirdi Baba and asked, 'Do I make this up or imagine all this or is this really happening, please give me a sign.' Suddenly the 'yellow' light on Baba's face started glowing and Shirdi Baba's eyes looked at me as though they were alive. I had my answer, this was not my imagination, but experiencing the presence of God. I can only state here how very much I love You the Babas, Jesus and my Shirdi Sai.

September

Another Strange Dream—My Shirdi Sai comes into My Life
I witnessed Radha organising a birthday party for me along with the other devotees of Shirdi Sai. He was his usual kind self, laying all the presents on a table, etc., but when I went to make a Thank You speech, I was interrupted by a lady there who presented me with a gross hat made of animal skins. I kept enquiring as to where Swami's picture was as I was disappointed in not seeing Him. I also noticed Shirin, Prasanna, Sai devotees and my friends from our bhajan group and Kala in another room, Prasanna wearing the most beautiful ruby earrings. We were then all handed out cards, I looked at mine only to see the Joker from Batman staring at me. I was upset that it was not Swami's face. Radha's daughter then showed me her card and there was an old man with a scarf around his head. I asked her who he was and if she would exchange pictures with me. But she held on tightly to her card saying, 'No it's my dad'. I looked puzzled as the man in her picture was too old to be Radha, the girl's father in real life. I know it was my Shirdi Baba, thank You for coming into my dream.

Bhajan (20 September)
Today is my first bhajan in this house. At aarti, Swami came, I begged Him to grace us with His divine presence tonight. I felt very agitated, anxious and nervous. I repeated, 'Have no fear, Swami is here'.

I asked Swami to keep the neighbours indoors. I laughed. There was a mild storm and they had to stay inside. Thank You Swami for Your small leela. It was 3 p.m. I was extremely nervous. None of the devotees of Swami have arrived yet to help put up the altar. Oh what a beautiful puja it turned out! Thank You my beloved Swami.

The group was small, Dr Vithi – a charmer, Radha, Badal, Sharma, Ajnani, Henry, Joy, Kala, Shirin, Rajesh, Jack – but it was so very beautiful. Rita did a stupendous job of setting up a very pretty and precious altar, such love and patience she has. Shirin was the master chef, Radha and Raj polished and scrubbed all the brassware. Such kind people—the food they cooked, the flowers and fruits brought, all turned out to be a very spiritual and enlightening evening. Dr Vithi, after puja and bhajans did Reiki. I simply loved Swami's gifts to me—His blessings on the house, the sweet orange, and the thread. I cherished every minute of the evening. I did my first and a brief aarti. We were all allowed to hold Swami's materialised gold lingam which belonged to Dr Vithi. We told our stories, ate the delicious food. Shirin was instructed by Swami to give me the sari worn by the altar, which was so beautiful. I was moved. At one stage of the bhajans, the tulips began to sway shaking their heads to the bhajans. Never fear, Swami was here, even though there were no fans or any breeze blowing to make the tulips nod.

October

My Birthday

At least one of my dreams came true—(refer to the dream witnessed in September where Radha's daughter had found a picture of an old man and when Shirdi Sai enters my life). Here is the reality of it. At bhajans today Rita told me that one of her daughters had received a picture of Shirdi Baba at some function. Everybody else received Swami's picture. I had dreamt of this. She showed me the picture it was the same I had seen in the dream, the old man with a scarf on His head, but instead of keeping it, like she did in the dream, she gave me the picture. This was the first little picture I had received of Shirdi Sai, my lifelong love, and that too on my birthday!

Dream

There was a tall, bald, pundit in a room along with a member of my family. He started talking and said something defamatory against Swami. I gave him a piece of my mind and told him in no uncertain terms never to speak of Swami like that again. I then looked at the altar, there were about four statues on it, they all started to move and shake vigorously and multiplied into about eight beautiful statues, before everyone's eyes. We all looked aghast and I shouted aloud to all, 'This is what my Swami just did, *never* speak *ill of Him*'. Two of the statues were very beautiful and were covered in white and gold. They glowed and I stated, 'Look He even brought Radha and Krishna'. This was the end of the first dream. I do not know how to interpret these dreams except to recall Baba's words in the *Sai Satcharita*, 'Never speak ill of others'.

Dream of Dreams

I saw Swami, so very handsome and young looking. My family and I were swarming around Swami. I was elated. Swami asked us all to sit in front. I could see myself so excited. I asked Swami, 'Swami, mother wants to know if I will get married again?' Swami replied, 'No, but you have other things to do'. I was visibly upset. Swami also said, 'You and your daughter will be close, don't worry, you will be okay'. I awoke and was puzzled. A very vivid dream, I heard Swami very clearly and saw Swami very vividly. After two hours of being awake, I fell back to sleep.

Another Dream. Same Night.

I saw myself looking at a picture. I thought I saw Swami in it, but on closer inspection Swami was not there. During the previous dream I also saw an Indian man shouting at Swami about a plot of land and graves. I called out to my sister Cheryl, who was upstairs, to rummage through the draws, find the papers and bring it down as requested by Swami. The man seemed very angry, Swami was nonplussed. The dream ended here.

I have not had darshan of beloved Swami/Shirdi at aarti and I feel totally devastated. I was reading *Thy Will Be Done*, the author surely got Swami's grace many times over! A lucky and blessed man! I enjoyed bhajans on Saturday with Kala (25 October). (Homebush is another suburb of Sydney, where bhajans are held once a month). The altar was beautifully and lovingly decorated. I loved the meditation session.

I had asked for a sign and was granted the same. I will now make my plans to travel to Puttaparthi. The sign given with Swami's grace being thus. On the way home on spending a lovely lunch with some friends, I asked again for a sign from Swami, i.e., if I should travel to India, namely Puttaparthi, did not even know of a place called Shirdi. I stepped into the train and sat down. The seat in front of me had the words 'Travel Travel Travel' etched on it, this was my sign. Thank You Swami. I look forward to the trip. You are allowing me to take.

****

When Lisa and I were in Calcutta in 1990, at that time again knowing nothing of Shirdi Sai or Sathya Sai, two incidents kept coming back to my mind today. One of importance was affirmed by my beloved Baba today, seven years later. In Calcutta, I was curious to visit a temple, never having entered one before. A very gracious and beautiful lady (Manju, a friend of the Verghese family, who lives in Calcutta, and the Verghese family, who we had travelled to India with) consented to show us around a temple. I also wanted Lisa to see what a Temple looked like and its contents. There were many gods/goddesses and a pundit at the main altar. A lady came in and handed the pundit a box of laddoos. He offered it to the gods and then turned around and offered it to Lisa and me, our first prasad. At the time we did not know what it meant and were hesitant to take the same, but the lady said, 'Take, it is an offering from the God' (Thanks Ganapati). Laddoos/Ganapati? Since this story I try to remember to offer Ganesha laddoos whenever I remember to do so, I know He loves them, so do I.

****

Lisa and I were in a taxi in Calcutta looking for a relatives house. As usual, Calcutta streets are hot, dirty and crowded. The taxi stopped at an address and we alighted. Much to our fear and annoyance, (fear because of the crowds), we could not find the place. Suddenly an old man with an umbrella appeared and asked if we needed help. I showed him the address. He very kindly sheltered us under his umbrella as it was raining and took us all the way to their door. His kindness brought tears to my eyes and I gave him Rs 5. On entering the door at the top of the staircase, I turned around once more to thank the old man, but he had disappeared as fast as he had appeared. I now know in my heart that was my Shirdi Baba (my first darshan/dakshina). I asked Baba at prayer this morning if indeed that was Him and it was affirmed. Many times in these past nine years, I meet people and in my heart I feel like I am looking or talking to Shirdi Sai.

December

In my dream (around 5.30 a.m.), I saw Lisa talking to a very handsome Indian, dressed all in white, and who looked rather sad.

I asked Shirdi Baba at aarti at 7.00 a.m. if it was Him? I got my reply. 'Yes'. My heart was joyful that my beloved Shirdi Baba had talked to Lisa.

1998

January

Dreams

In my dream (2 January), I kept seeing all these men looking like my Shirdi Sai and I kept making comments like 'no he is not wearing his scarf on the left side', etc. I guess my joy at journeying to India soon to see my Baba was beginning to show.

****

On 26 January, I dreamt that I was in a room with Jenny my cousin, who handed me a picture of Shirdi Baba saying that she prayed to Him, and He emerged in person before her. I immediately went on my knees and begged Shirdi Baba to do the same for me. Nothing happened in the dream but I prayed that it will happen in reality for me.

****

In another dream, I saw everything as a blue haze, when I noticed Swami wearing a blue gown. I don't recall what Swami said (my excitement gets the better of me, even in dreams), but Swami looked very young. The place looked like an Ashram with ladies sitting everywhere. Swami walked up to an angelic but sick-looking child on a stretcher, all dressed in white and blessed her. I then saw myself carrying the mail, and Kala told me I had to present it to Swami. Again, I was extremely excited about approaching Swami. The dream ended.

****

I prayed to Swami for a cheque so that I could pay for the trip. I received money from Lisa along with a beautiful card with an imprint of Lord Ganesha on it. He removed the money obstacle or lack of it and paid for the ticket.

February

My First Trip to Shirdi/Puttaparthi

I had a pinch of vibhuti at the airport to calm the nerves. Sitting near a set of very noisy twins in the plane, I had to intone Swami to give the poor mother some relief. She looked a wreck. Alas, they had fallen asleep. Thanks Swami. There was mild turbulence, I was going to start my *Aums*. Turbulence had stopped and I felt peaceful again.

Mumbai/Shirdi

You can't see the sky for the pollution. They have some beautiful buildings, if only they cleaned the same. I was invited for a delicious lunch and warm hospitality by Shirin's mother. I then drove down to Shirdi. I was in a state of abject shock on the road—the honking, merging, ducking and weaving of every conceivable vehicle, but it was admirable to see the respect that each driver gave to the other. No road rage here only 'spot on' hand signals. The scenery was quite awesome, the beautiful mountain ranges, the magnificent sunset. It was very arid and hot, but I loved India and with tears I drove into Shirdi, my first ever visit. At the entrance of the hotel 'Sai Leela', the grand old man, Shirdi Sai was there to greet His guests. I longed for the picture. It was 3.30 a.m. and I had not yet fallen asleep as there was a lizard on the wall, and I could not stop being afraid of it. It was looking at me and I at it. Shirdi Sai is it You, tick ticking on the wall, watching over me?

Shirdi Sansthan (4 February)

I bought flowers and a thali for Shirdi Sai. The place was filthy, overcrowded (remember this was my first trip and my first impressions), a commercial paradise for street vendors. I did not understand anything that was happening. Just did a *namaskaram* to Baba and I left. I was happy to see the beautiful murti of Baba, but very uncomfortable with the crowds, so quickly I left, in tears. I realised that I love Shirdi Sai, even though I do not know much about Him. It feels like my heart and soul have gone out to Him. I cannot understand this strange feeling come over me for Shirdi Sai, nor explain this strange connection.

I left Shirdi at 9.15 a.m. and met with a minor car accident. Perhaps I should have taken leave of Shirdi Sai, but not knowing how He thinks at this stage, He had shown me His first sign of greatness. We ended up at a police station and after much debate, we were told to go on. Thank You Shirdi Sai for this first trip to Shirdi. I pray it is not my last.

Back in Mumbai, I did a tour of the city. I was very impressed with the architecture of the old buildings (even though dirty) like VT, Gateway of India, the Taj Hotel. I stayed at a hotel called 'The Godwin', God won I didn't. It was a stinky room. I had to ask them to place me in another room. Utterly exhausted, I could not sleep for the stench. I decided to wake up, and I observed from the hotel window a beautiful *surya* (sun) rise. I took many photos. After an American breakfast Mani, my hired driver (a lovely chap) decided to show me the sights of Mumbai before the flight to Parthy. The buildings appeared to me quaint in architecture; if only they were maintained and cleaned. I was sad to farewell Mani. He was a humble gem of a man (and a good driver too).

I was sitting at the Mumbai airport with stomach cramps. 'Okay Swami, I have no medication but You can help, please do,' I said to myself. He did, the cramps stopped, but we had to wait very long owing to plane delays and disruptions. It was 2.30 p.m., and we were still waiting; our patience was being severely tested. This was my first trip. I did not know what lay ahead? Yes, this is India. At 2.50 p.m. we were ready to fly. It was a good flight, but made a bad landing. I was waiting for a porter at Parthy airport to carry the bags, only to be told by another passenger that I had to do it myself. No Swami, I can't lift anything over a kilogram. Oh! We Westerners do expect a lot, I do. Swami heard my cry for help and sent a kind chap and his wife from Canada (Ramesh and Manju), to help me in my struggle and He lifted my case for me.

Puttaparthi (5 February)

At the Ashram, I was expecting a room to myself (not knowing anything at this stage of how things work here, and amazed by the surge of people gathered in and around a large hall). I had to share with a lady from Venezuela (Ruth), a South American model. Another test for me, vanity. I wished I could look as glamorous as Ruth, Baba on the other hand, preferred the plain Jane look for me. After dropping the suitcase in the room I ran to the hall, where there was something going on. I could not get in but noticed Swami's hair. He was bringing in the Chinese New Year. I was very excited and kept jumping up and down at the back, just to see *the hair*; this darshan (5 February) was enough for me. Back to the room for a cold shower (Oh God! More testing; never had a cold shower in my life). But it was refreshing.

First Darshan – Poonachandra (6 February)

I sat for hours like the rest, the legs and back were killing me, but one was not allowed to move or go out, as one learnt the Seva Dal rules fast here. I called them the Seva Mafia (readers please share my humour here), as this was all that it meant to me at that time. I did not know their worthiness at this initial stage. Swami appeared at 7.00. He was too far away, but I was very grateful to be here at His Lotus Feet. He walked ever so gracefully. I was thrilled to witness the materialisation of vibhuti by Swami for a lucky Chinese lady. It was my first darshan and it was awesome. I made my way to the Western canteen where I met this very beautiful lady (Anuradha) who for some reason reminded me of Shirdi Baba. We started to chat and she told me she was from Burma, where my mother and her mother came from. Anu had been staying here since 1968. I loved her instantly. Bhajans were beautiful and on the way out I was grateful to have a full frontal darshan of Swami. More tears were coming out of my eyes. I love You Swami. After the darshan at noon, I found fifty rupees lying on the road on the way to my room. I was a bit surprised as there were so many people walking in this area and no one had spotted it. I felt I was meant to pick it up, which I did. This has been lying in my prayer room since and still is.

Lisa's Birthday (7 February)

Today is my daughter Lisa's birthday. May she be blessed today and always. Arrived early in time for Suprabhatam, it was awesome. I got the eighth row. The chanting of the mantras that early in the morning, the stillness was just so very beautiful. I had a brief darshan of Swami, but that was bliss in itself for me. Swami, please shower extra blessings on Lisa today. After breakfast I went for orientation, and thoroughly enjoyed the talk. I learnt something new about the Ashram, that one had to buy coupons for the South Indian canteen. There were long queues. Yes, patience was being taught here. I decided to have a massage. I found a lady outside the Ashram who was willing to give massage inside the Ashram.

Lakshmi was her name. She came to the room and doused me with oil from head to foot, I stank but she was good. She also chatted about the three gowns she had received from Swami. I became a little green with envy here, wishing for even a sleeve from Swami. Maybe one day. After she left, I realised there was no hot water. Well, this oiled body just stayed in the room till the oil came off; I had many *cold* sponges later.

8 February

Today is Sunday. I had a throbbing headache. I had a beautiful darshan. Swami spent a long time with the crowds handing out things. At one stage I thought Swami would walk down our line, He was so close, but He turned and went on. I was disheartened but was grateful for the darshan. I love You Swami. My lucky roommate Rutha and her fellow Venezuelans got an interview with Swami. They were also given a japamala by Swami.

Today we got the last line, I have much to bear. I came back to the room after darshan and could not stop crying. I just felt very sad. I missed my Shirdi Sai here. I met Manju and Ramesh and we did a tour of some interesting places, the Museum, the Samadhis of Swami's parents, and the Wishfulfilling tree, which was so awesome and very spiritual for me. I cried a lot. From Swami's place of birth, I picked up some sand and a fruit growing there. I met Swami's nephew who invited us to come back to his home at night. I also met Swami's brother, but he did not give us vibhuti. One of the other men there told us to return that night. I magically ran into my travel agent from Australia, Indu and her husband Shekar, who were in Parthy for a brief visit. Good to see familiar faces from Australia. Though I still didn't know too much about Shirdi Sai, I was very happy to see a large portrait of Him on entering the North Indian canteen. I seemed to miss Him a great deal though I still didn't know too much about Shirdi Sai.

I got the sixth row today. It was the last day for me and I was very sad to leave. I got an excellent darshan of Swami. I could almost reach out and touch Him. Good to see Him so close. Thank You Swami (and my Shirdi Sai) for bringing me to Your Divine Lotus Feet. Thanks to all the lovely people that I came in contact with while here in Puttaparthi.

Bangalore

It was my first visit to Bangalore in many years. It brought back happy memories of when I was in my teens and lived with the Brigidine nuns in Bangalore. I checked into 'Quality Inn'. It was so good to have a hot shower; no more oily body. The food and service was excellent. I gorged on 'Veg Karti's', sweet lassi and rasmalai and had a tummy ache. Served me right for being greedy.

Mysore (11 February)

Another horrific drive but the rural areas were beautiful and lush. I stopped for a *dab*, bought a lotus, and then visited Tipu Sultan's Palace with a guide in tow. There were impressive gardens (except for the stagnant pools and ponds), the Palace was structurally super for its age. No cameras were allowed in though. This was a pity, as to film the frescoes inside, the teak constructions and the stucco, would have made wonderful prints, and I was not going to settle for a postcard. Then I drove to the Hagallappa's Place, the Sai Orphanage. It was very poorly maintained, and the place was smelling of urine just outside the mandir. A little girl opened it for me. A pundit came in and performed a short puja, gave me vibhuti and amrit. I cried for having received so much of amrit on my hands produced from the Sai lockets. I could not swallow it all, so I forgot and rubbed some on my hair, but was surprised that the hair did not get sticky, it just melted into the hair, a miracle. The hands too, though were not washed appeared just clean and clear. A Sai leela indeed! Thanks Baba.

I toured around Mysore, the Maharaja's Palace (what a palace and one part is still occupied by the Maharaja's son!), St. Philomena's beautiful church, was absolutely a magnificent architecture (reminded me of Gaudi's La Sagrada Famile in Barcelona) where again photography was prohibited, and went down to the catacombs where there was a replica of St. Philo. As a child I was confirmed with St. Philiomena's name upon making my Confirmation in school. I lit some candles for the family. Then, I received darshan of Shirdi Sai in a shop, and was very happy. After a lovely day and delicious dinner, the dreaded thought of returning back to Australia the next day hit me. Depression was setting in, I did not want to leave. Before departure, I visited the Shirdi Baba Temple in Cambridge Layout. There was a large crowd. I paid my respects, and one of the pundits gave me a huge garland of roses.

Thank You my beloved Shirdi Sai. I took one of the roses from it and had to leave the rest of the garland with the driver, pity I could not bring it to Australia. Thank You for the first trip Baba, keep them coming for me please.

March

Dreams

In my dream, I saw myself standing besides two elephants, one being extremely large, of gargantuan proportions, the other a baby which I picked up and hugged. I was being led by a guide through a palace where large ornate doors opened, (in reality I saw this door at the Mysore Palace on my first trip to Parthy). I could hear the chanting of '*Sai Sai*' and bhajans, women were taking their places for darshan, waiting expectantly. One of the doors opened and I saw *the hair* hoping it to be Swami. I looked up to see a balcony where a pundit appeared, showering very heavy, thick incense on the guide and me, which I ingested and at the same time yelling out 'come to me Swami, come to me'. I then heard a roar and turning around saw this beautiful old wooden carriage being drawn by horses with footmen at the rear, (in reality I saw the palki procession on a Thursday in Shirdi), entering the palace. I realised they were there to escort Swami in. I quickly headed towards the darshan line and sat besides the other ladies. Sadly, I then awoke.

****

In my dream, I saw Cheryl (my sister) and myself and two boys at a concert hall in boxed seats. I was as usual talking about Baba and Cheryl left. Then I saw a picture at my feet. Noticing it to be Shirdi Baba, I said to the boys, 'I called Baba and He came', but on looking closely at the picture I noted it not to be Shirdi Baba but a very tall God with a trident in his hand, who looked like a Yogi. Somebody then whispered in my ear 'Look at the golden tears in the picture'. I awoke. Was it Shiva?

****

In my dream, I was in a very dark room or tunnel looking for Baba. I kept calling for Baba, but it was very dark. Then I saw myself with two Indian girls. They were about to have injections and I was telling the doctor that he should use smaller syringes. Next I heard a bhajan and I started singing, stating happily, this is a Sai bhajan. I closed my eyes in concentration and meditation trying to picture Baba, but I could clearly visualise a man in a turban, my Shirdi Baba. Same morning, I did my readings, sat talking to Baba and the Divine Light shone. I know now how the children felt at Lourdes and Fatima. I can only state here how much I longed for and loved Baba. This has been one of the best days in my life.

****

I was in the middle of reading *Life Is A Dream – Realise It* by Joy Thomas. She was very blessed by Swami. I had my own dream where I saw a man selling different aarti deepaks – so I was pleased to be able to do aarti at Kala's bhajans. Also, I had a dream seeing Radha watering his garden when another chap entered the home and said, 'Oh Swami, I have heard of Him', which made me ecstatic. This was the end of my dream.

Strange Occurrences

I spent the afternoon reading *Lokanatha Sai*. I was so very happy to experience the fragrance of vibhuti that was coming through once or twice while reading!

****

I took a red and white rose from the bhajans session held at Kala's residence. The next day the white rose had withered so I let it face Swami's picture and said to the rose, 'Hold your head high and look at Swami'. That was on Friday morning, today is Sunday, the rose is proudly, head still erect, looking at our Swami. To end on a humorous note, before going to bed last night I said to Swami, 'If and when I think, say and do anything bad or wrong, correct me immediately so that I may not do so again'. During the course of a dream about a colleague, I could see myself just about to berate him in some way when I was awakened immediately by a throbbing little finger. I spoke aloud – 'Thank You Swami for reminding me, but don't make it so severe next time'. Then I went back to sleep.

****

Last week, while in bed, I had a traumatic and painful spasm. I prayed to Baba to help me, as I knew this could be quite agonising as I get it often enough. I was lying on my side when I felt intense heat from the stomach and also around the painful area, then something very heavy on me was trying to tear out whatever pain was there. I was baffled. The pain disappeared. This really happened to me in my bed at home and I was awake. It was no dream.

Sai Humour

I was reading *Sai Satcharita* yesterday. To quote Shirdi Baba, 'even if you call upon my bones, they will come to you'. Before retiring for the night I retorted to Shirdi Sai 'then let your bones come to me and let me see them', I started laughing then fell off to sleep. Early this morning I had a dream. I saw a large gathering of ladies with a microphone blaring the bhajan 'Raghupati Raghava'. I started yelling 'Swami is coming, Swami is coming' and we all promptly sat down for bhajans. Lisa, mother and nana were also in attendance. Lisa was complaining that she did not know who Swami was, and did not want to be there. I told her to leave and she did. Mother was talking loudly, I told her to be quiet and respectful. Nana looked confused. I was trying to impress mother by singing a Sanskrit bhajan, though I was completely elated that Baba was coming.

I then noticed near me, an extremely *gaunt, bony*, emaciated looking lady trying to light the aarti. She looked at me and although she was a woman, had the face of Shirdi Baba. This was end of the dream. I awoke and turned on the light and laughed at Baba's picture near my bed saying, 'that was *You*, the *bones*', wasn't it?

At prayer this morning in my puja room, I asked Shirdi Baba, 'I did dream about the bones last night, I know it was *You*, please give me a sign so that I may pen it in my diary'. He did. I had an absolutely fabulous darshan, even Swami's face flashed bright – the sight of God is so beautiful, bones and all Baba's omnipresence was made clear to me last night.

****

In another dream, I saw all the ladies at the Centre were together picking up and clearing dishes after a meal. I picked up a brass goblet and Prasanna, Sai devotee from our bhajan group, who passed away sadly last year, and a good friend to all, turned to me and said, 'that will have to be cleaned 24 times'. I started polishing the same and counting at the same time. Then I saw a picture of Swami very high on a wall, right in the corner. I could clearly see Swami's hair, but Swami's face was covered entirely with a thick foam or paint. I climbed a ladder nearby and tried every effort to remove the paint so that I could see Swami. I awoke.

I continued thinking about the goblet – its cleaning for 24 times; Swami covered and me trying to uncover. I was baffled by this dream.

Baba's Love

Oh bliss is with me. At puja this morning I stated, before japa, 'Baba, I will only smile if I see Your Divine Light, so please let it shine on me.' I finished my prayers and decided to do japa in the lounge as the smell of the incense was too strong in the puja room. Oh bliss, my smile broadened and I beamed as the Divine Light shone ever so brightly for almost half an hour. I thanked Thee Baba for Thy kindness and compassion. On my way to Minto for an interview, the car next to the taxi I was travelling in was BA-1. I had to laugh, Baba was accompanying me for a job interview.

****

Off to another interview and on the way I uttered to Baba, 'if You care for me, show me a rainbow'. I scanned the heavens to and fro but nothing appeared. I was even more disappointed for not being successful at getting a job. Just before retiring for the night, there was a commercial on TV and though I am one who doesn't normally pay much attention to commercials on TV, my attention was caught by the biggest rainbow in the commercial. Thank You Baba, You do care for me.

****

When one asks for Baba's guidance, be mindful of it and follow through. It was 9.23 a.m. I had a shower and the brain was back to normal. I began 'rapid recall', be patient, saburi. While I was doing noon aarti, I noticed Swami's Lotus Feet, the Light shone briefly from them but at one stage, they looked like that there was a ripple going through them and as if Swami was walking or was about to walk. I also noticed a Light emanating from a small picture of Shirdi Baba, very brief though.

I realised that I was panicking about a job and my financial situation, but that there was a reason why I was being rejected at interviews. I went to hospital next week for a day, prior to this I had to fast for three days. I see this as Baba's guidance and sign to me that I should first take care of my health and then think about a job. I was happy once again, my anxiety had left me, I knew my Baba was always with me and He will be giving me the right job at the right time.

I was having a cup of coffee and staring out of the window. We only get mynah birds here, but noticed this tiny little blue bird dancing around merrily on the fence. It looked so happy, I was enchanted by its colour. The bird was a little larger than a sparrow but its colour was awesome. It was bright blue with black stripes. I admired its beauty and said to myself, 'the blue bird of happiness'. Padma, another Sai Devotee, rang me this morning regarding Sydney ` (a group who help people in distress over the telephone). I was a part of it for a few months and Padma used to ring me to tell me what time and day I would be on call duty which I will be doing tomorrow. We spoke at length about Swami and I told her about the blue bird. She immediately said that it was Lord Krishna.

I was very disturbed still being jobless. I had been housing a Uni student who I found was slow and lazy. My anger had resurfaced. Besides reading a book *Messages from My Baba* by Elvie Bailey had not helped me one bit. She had claimed that for every breath she took including that of her blessed family, Swami was for ever at her call. I only desired the same. I asked Swami to help me and show Himself in some way as I was in utter despair last night. I had a quick dream this morning. I was staring at a very beautiful lady dressed all in white 'like brilliant glowing white'. She said something to me, but I never understood her as there were people around stating 'the war has started'. The lady disappeared and I found myself getting angry that everybody was unperturbed about the war, they went on doing what they were doing. I then saw myself crawling on a wooden plank. My dream came to an end. When I awoke I remembered the lady in white. At prayer that morning I asked Shirdi Baba, 'Was that *You* in Your kafni?' I got my answer. The *Light*. I was so very joyful to see The Divine Light shining brightly at prayer, especially Thy Eyes and Thy Lotus Feet; also a few flashes and Shirdi Baba's flesh in the face.

August

12 August

Let me feel Thy Presence, Let me see Thy Presence, and oh joy! I did. At noon aarti Baba's beautiful eyes shone and glowed, and the Divine Light shone through them. Blessed are the meek for they shall see God. I feel so meek and humble and so loved/blessed by Baba, though not that I am meek or humble.

13 August

I got up in a very peaceful mood in the morning. I was very pleased for doing the meditation and prayers. As usual, I kept badgering Baba for His grace and leelas. At aarti in the morning, Baba's eyes looked so blessed and beautiful, I was mesmerised. The Divine Light glowed with full force, I wanted only to continue to see God, feel God, hear God, touch God and love God. I must add that Shirdi Baba's picture and the beloved Lotus Feet of the Swami glowed too.

14 August

The next day I should have been calm after the beautiful darshan from Baba's pictures. At last I saw the small Lotus Feet light up, and as for Shirdi Baba – I could have grabbed Him. His eyes winked and His face was aglow. But I was very stressed with the student living with me, for the water he wasted. Baba I can't handle this side of things very well, I would, with Your help, like to stay centred on You, but am finding it very difficult to do so. Please detach me from this situation. Okay Shirdi Baba, I just got a flashback of You and the lepers, *Sai Ram*. I shall try to be tolerant to the boy's ways, with Your help.

****

Yes, I am indeed blessed. After reading, enjoying, crying and loving *Shri Sai Baba*, written by V.B. Kher (translator) I lay down, feeling the heat of the sun. It was 11.00 a.m. I turned to Shirdi Baba's picture by the bedside and was talking to Him about the garland at Bangalore that I had received from the pujari with *green eyes*. I said, 'Baba was the pujari *You*, if so, I received the garland from *Your* hands and I have but one rose petal left, which I treasure'. The picture *glowed, the Divine Light shone, I cried*. Shirdi Baba answered me. *I had darshan of my beloved Shirdi Baba. He was* the pujari. The darshan that I received from the little picture was awesome. The Light covered the whole picture for quite a while so that I could not see Baba's face at all, and saw just the Light. *Koti koti pranaams Baba.*

****

I was sitting in the lounge reading a book. I asked Baba, 'I would like the garland back' and I immediately got the most beautiful smell of roses. While writing this, I got a call saying I did not get the job at Mediclinic. I was disappointed, but I left it to Baba to guide me and give me the right job.

17 August

After aarti in the morning, I went back to bed. The door of the puja room was ajar and I had a perfect view of the first two pictures of Swami and Shirdi Baba. Shirdi Baba's picture gave such wondrous darshan. The face kept changing very quickly to Guru Nanak, Gandhi and particularly Hanuman, which I saw quite clearly and many times, and then a very *young handsome Shirdi Baba*. This went on for quite a long while, at least fifteen minutes. Is this some sort of a message to me? I tried to go back to sleep and I felt the *Divine warmth*. I felt so secured and loved and no more alone, delighted but also a little timid of Baba's beautiful darshan. I love Thee my Baba (I even ignored the student's long shower today).

Dream (18 August)

Early morning, around 4.30 a.m., I had a dream. I saw *my grand old man Shirdi Sai Baba*, standing with a group of people. He was wearing His white kafni. I was crying and telling Him not to go. He looked at me gently and comforted me. I awoke. At aarti I asked Shirdi Baba, 'if that really was *You* please give me a sign so that I may tell others'. On looking at Shirdi Baba's picture His eyes first blinked and I saw this 'puff of smoke' (probably from His chillum) which hit my face and I moved by head back. Baba, what was happening? (Reader, please note before I write these 'special events', I always ask Baba if I may write the same. So this is Baba's Divine Hand that writes the same, not mine.) *Koti Koti pranaams Baba.* The darshans (that's what I refer them to) occur in the puja room.

25 August

A bit gloomy morning. There was no darshan. After aarti, while I was waiting for the student to leave, Shirdi Baba did *the face changing*. Oh how I love Thee my Baba. At noon aarti, Shirdi Baba's eyes kept blissfully blinking and on the other picture, the eyes actually became so real, I got a bit scared. I asked Baba if I could start typing a book, the answer was 'No'. I then asked (casting lots) if I could continue to write in the diary, the answer was 'Yes'. Thank You Baba/Swami.

****

In my dream I saw myself making a collage. A small packet fell onto the collage. I picked it up and noted it to be a packet of vibhuti. With much joy I stuck it to the collage and completed the same. Also at aarti this morning, I asked for concentration. I received it in the most beautiful vision! I saw a large statue of Ganapati in a deep cave with a light shining in the background. Quite beautiful!

This morning during bhajans, all the ladies were dressed in their best silk sarees. I was told by Shirin, a Sai devotee from our bhajan group, that it was a Ganapati festival. Maybe, one day with Baba's grace, I will become more involved with this spiritual side of things and perhaps gain more insight in Hindu gods and goddesses. I was grateful for the vision of Lord Ganesh yesterday.

****

Early morning around 5.30/6.00 a.m., I had this dream. Before going to bed last night, I was distressed and said to Baba, 'Regarding my life – if You are taking care of this for me, give me a sign, I don't know what to do any more, and I will recognise the sign if You do'. With that I fell into a deep sleep. I awoke at 4 a.m. and did japa/meditation and fell back to deep sleep. In my dreams I saw myself complaining to the family who were standing at my front door, in hushed tones, about the student. I was pretending that he had left, when he was actually sitting at the dining table. The room was very dark. The friends left and when I entered the dining area I was aghast to see the student covered in vibhuti and here was a mound of it on the table. I just looked at it with my mouth agape. I then saw a street scene where I was playing with a ferret. There was a line of boys with vibhuti in their hands. Their teacher was explaining to them that this was a spiritual house and I saw them toss the vibhuti on to the walls. I went into the house and saw my uncle telling us to vacate the house as it was electrified. I was trying to question him if he had seen Baba in the house or was it Baba that he was mistaking for electricity. The dream came to an end.

****

It has happened twice now and both times when it was very dark. I was awake around 3.00 a.m. and just like I see the White Cloud that sometimes comes over the pictures, a white cloud was hovering all over the bedroom. The first time I saw it I thought my eyes were tired, but I saw it very clearly today. I was afraid as I thought of Casper the Friendly Ghost, but once I got accustomed to it, I hid no more under the sheets, realising it was Baba sending

Angels in this form as a protection. I asked Baba at aarti this morning if the 'Ghost' was indeed Him—'Yes' was the answer. He gives me a sign which I seemed to understand.

September

7 September

On meditation this morning I felt as though my neck was being healed by Baba. My whole head and right side of the neck and shoulder became very hot. I mentioned to Baba the intensity of the heat, and the very next minute there was a cool breeze being fanned across my face.

The ghostly angelic cloud was in the bedroom again. It was really fluttering and flying all over the place and appeared quite large. I felt as though my body was levitating and was blissful. When I rang Padma (one of the Sydney Samaritans who are a group of volunteers who counsel people in grief over the phone) for handover of the night shift in the morning, I mentioned about the cloud. She said it was an angel (Baba in that form) and a form of protection. I was very happy.

Thank You Baba (13 September)

I know how *You* performed two miracle cures for me: (1) the ulcers, when Shirdi Baba removed the *force* from my stomach (dream written earlier) and (2) when *You* touched my neck (energy dream). One day if it be *Thy Will*, these leelas may be written in a book. Also before beginning aarti, I was getting flashes from the altar and then I had a very beautiful and 'full darshan' from my Baba.

The Cancer Story (25 September)

On 11 September, I went into day surgery at Campbelltown hospital for a pharynx, laryngoscopy and oesophogoscopy, as the right side of my throat was found to be very inflamed and had constant bleeding (I had nasopharyngeal carcinoma in 1980 and was treated with surgery and radiotherapy). I have been well all these years and was rather alarmed when my throat started bleeding again. I presumed that the cancer had returned.

My family and friends were all very upset and concerned as we all had bad/sad memories of past eighteen years. Di and I spent the week in phone conversations and she has always been my 'tower of strength', ever caring and sharing my joys and sorrows, and we seem to be very spiritually linked. Two hours before I left for the hospital, Di, being ever so kind, had rung me but the two of us were so sad that we just cried. So I promised Di that I would ring her when I was out of the hospital.

In the hospital the examinations went well with the only panic being that my BP rose to 222 degrees! I could see the alarm on the faces of the nursing team and I could hear them say, 'Relax Lorraine relax, your BP is too high'. I also noticed I was wearing an oxygen mask and I tried in vain to remove it, but the team would not allow me to as I had a lot of trouble breathing.

The staff at Recovery kept monitoring my BP repeating 'Relax Lorraine'. Finally, when I was able to think a little clearer when the anaesthetic was wearing away, I asked Baba/Swami to please bring my BP down. Immediately, it started falling. I was released at 7.45 p.m. but was told *not* to speak for twenty-four hours and to return to Casualty if I had a breathing problem. At this stage I thanked dear Kala and Raj for all their help and support in taxiing me to and from the hospital, and being my very dear friends and support in my time of need. Thank you Kala and Raj and Di too.

I slept peacefully that night as upon leaving the hospital the doctor confirmed to me that there was *No Cancer* but I would get the final results in two weeks after the biopsies were returned from the laboratory. I thank *You* Baba.

The next day Di rang but I could barely whisper to her 'No cancer'. She replied, 'I know'. I whispered, 'How?' She said that after our last conversation on Friday at about 9.30 p.m., she was going from her car to work when she distinctly heard Swami say, 'no cancer – something else'. As usual Di ever curious asked Swami, what else. 'Salience'. On entering her office, one of her staff wished her and said, 'I have such a sore throat today – must be ulcers or lesions'. Di got her answer from Baba, and I had mine, I should be silent. When I do talk, I talk too much. Now You have to teach me to be *Salience. Sai Ram.*

****

I had my follow-up appointment today (25 September), I knew my Baba had healed me a few days prior to the hospital (refer to healing date: 7 September). Results – Absolutely clear, no bleeding no cancer. Nothing short of a miracle that was! Thank You my Baba.

Dream

I **s**aw a temple, more like a stupa, with the word Shiva on it and a trident next to it. The dream ended here. On waking up I heard three distinct hisses like that of a snake, I even put the light on as I became a little alarmed. Before falling back to sleep I heard another hiss. I looked at Shirdi Baba's picture. I went back to sleep but kept hearing *Shiva, Shiva, Shiva Mahashivaratri*. I awoke. I had another dream of my beloved Shirdi. I don't remember the full dream except that I very clearly saw Shirdi Baba with full orange kafni and scarf. My joy at seeing Baba as large as life, so clearly and so close, woke me up.

October

12 October

It started last night. I kept getting a very strong smell of amrit, I thought it was the flowers, but the smell kept coming in bursts. It lasted for over an hour and at times was extremely strong. Feeling very happy I awoke around 10.30 (thanks to the neighbours being so loud outside) and started to panic about not falling back to sleep again as I had to attend three job interviews on the next day. I looked up at Shirdi above my bed and asked for His blessings. I wasn't awake for long after that, but as the light was on I was awoken a short time later by the sound of the most beautiful flute playing. Thank You Lord Krishna. I was then lulled into a fitful sleep.

****

After having meditated in the morning, I asked my Lord Baba to fill my every breath with His presence and to let the glorious day be specially full of His Divine leelas. I did get the smell of vibhuti on waking and at prayer. I felt more joy. My Baba blinked a couple of times and even though brief, the Light of my Lord Baba shone strongly from some of the pictures. It was 7.30 a.m. and I anticipated a day filled with my Baba. These feelings just come over me. Indeed the day turned out to be *odd*. I ended up rushing to Bankstown hospital in a cab for my first job interview which did not go too well. I did not do the test as I was rushing to the second interview at Liverpool hospital, forty-five minutes away from Bankstown. I had to board another taxi, more money was spent and I was late for the interview, but the panel waited for me. The test was not difficult. The third interview also went well except for the rostered hours and pay that I would have to endure. The best part came at Liverpool station. After a day of anxiety, hunger, etc., I ran down the platform as the train just pulled in, got into the carriage and was about to sit down when John Donnelly (a dear Swami devotee and an attendant on City Rail) hailed out to me to go into his train cabin which I did. My face lit up when I saw a picture of our beloved Swami and Lord Krishna. It was good to have a short satsang with John and his mate Mark about our Swami. This was my moment of bliss for the day. When the train stopped at Minto I saw Pushpa. Again I was delighted to see another Swami devotee. A sign perhaps, i.e., a job perhaps!

18 October

Neville Fredericks, a prominent Sathya Sai devotee and spokesman, spoke of our beloved Swami at a function today. Neville truly is blessed and clearly loves Swami. He was of gentle speech and manner, telling us of his first encounter with Swami, the lingam and the ring given to him by Swami and the story of the beggar. Most of all he cleared up a lot of things for me about love, loving oneself first; (after all God is housed in one's body temple) making at least five people happy every day, beginning with one's family and friends.

Spiritually, one should climb slowly (especially the Westerners) trying not to do all at once, as it won't be done well. One should do *one* thing but to be done well, i.e., through meditation. He spoke of love and I loved His spirituality. I actually attempted to sing a bhajan today with the group. I thought to myself, 'Give it a miss Lorraine, Gods will that you *don't sing* bhajans, leave it to the experts'.

20 October

What a night it was! After much tossing and turning and warding off moths, I fell into a fitful slumber to dream of myself being in a dilapidated train without a ticket, then being in a marketplace, and yes, I was even off the train and was riding an elephant! Got off to view all the hawkers selling Indian sweets and I remembered it was

Deepavali. Then I saw myself in my bedroom, lying on the bed and noticed that the clock was on the opposite side where I could see a shadow on the clock. I then felt two large heavy hands coming down on my back and the heat was intense. It was also trying to lift me. I looked up and saw two hands only, doing an Indian dance. I got so scared as the hands were approaching me and I yelled very loudly, '*Sai Ram, Sai Ram*'. I awoke yelling '*Sai Ram*'. I went back to sleep and awoke at 5.45 a.m. My back was very warm, like it was on fire. Baba!!! I forgot to mention the Divine Light shining on the photo of Jesus and the godesses (i.e., Lakshmi) in the puja room which I could see from my bed on waking.

November

Funny, Funny, Funny Baba (22 November)

You never let us do wrong by another (especially if a Sai devotee). John Donnelly gave me a tape on Mantra Meditation, but I really could not get 'into it', so I decided to tape some Sundaram Bhajans over it, thereby utilising the tape. At four attempts the recording button would not go down. I tried again today after bhajans, it would not tape, then decided to use another old tape, *Ram Ram Ram*, this one worked. Baba did not want me to tape something over John's kindness to me. You don't mess with Baba.

Funnier (26 November)

I decided to play and tape bhajans, trying once again to use that tape (John's). It would not move. I then replaced it with another, this worked. The Baba's 'no' is 'no'.

A Leela (29 November)

Utter confusion at the moment. The fridge stopped working on 26 November, all the contents became rancid and I threw all out. I was bewailing the failure of this expensive appliance complaining of my difficulties to my family and friend, i.e., no milk, no breakfast, etc., and oh how we depend on modern gadgets (wish I was at Swami's Gokulum, milk straight from the cows udder would have done me, with Swami's approval of course). Anyway, I went out yesterday and bought a new fridge which will be delivered next Saturday (5 December). Lo and behold! Before attending bhajans this morning, the old fridge started to work again. To cancel or not to cancel—I didn't cancel, so the new fridge was also delivered.

After bhajans, the last for the year, I went to Kalas to get the mail. Walking back home I got the most precious smell of vibhuti. Oh joy! On writing this paragraph, I again smelled the fragrance of vibhuti but ever so softly. The Babas were here.

December

4 December

I had an awful night after trying to keep from vomiting. The brain was tired and could function in front of a computer which I used all day at work. I was very anxious when told to page, to take patients away. My self-esteem was below zero, I had no confidence. How can the Babas ignore all this and not help? Even Ganesha doesn't seem to remove the obstacles. I am lost, afraid, anxious and ever so depressed. At morning aarti I could barely stand for lack of sleep, though I managed to do it and was pleased to see just a tad of Light. Short, but oh so good to see! I should be grateful for small mercies. Divine Light shone upon me.

8 December

Bliss, bliss, Divine bliss. At morning prayers I had not smiled (nay *beamed*) so brightly and broadly since weeks. The Lord's Divine Light shone in full on most of the pictures and for a long long time (I never wanted it to stop) and as for my little 'spectre on the wall'. He looked like there was a cloud in front of Him. Thank You Baba. May Thy Divine Light ever shine on me and mine. I forgot to mention, that I had asked Baba to give me a leela that morning on waking. Baba, what a leela 'Spectre on the wall'—Shirdi Sai can very clearly be seen by me in His white kafni, sitting in His usual pose, the left leg crossing over the right and even wearing His scarf. This image of Him is on the brick wall in my puja room.

A Fine Romance and Other Little Stories

I sent Swami a card for His Birthday and Christmas, letters, etc. I grumbled and complained all week to Swami that He never replies to my letters. It pays to grumble sometimes even to Swami. Here are Swami's pleasantries that occurred during this week.

I received Henry and Kala's card from Prashanti, my neighbours and devotees of Swami who were on holiday in Puttaparthi not directly from Swami, but it came from that soil and was written in Prashanti Nilayam (PN), Swami's abode.

It was Thursday morning (17 December). I was fast asleep for once; the next thing I remembered was being woken up to the words spoken very gently in my ear, but clearly, *Sai Sai Sai*. I woke up smiling.

22 December

After another week of utter sadness at Lisa not being with me for X-mas, (since she has been in Europe for a few years), I woke up with a tight chest and tears and loud sobs, crying my tales of woe to Baba. Half an hour later, I received a call from Lisa and we had a 'chit-chat' regarding her trip to Australia, etc. The highlight of the conversation was at the end when I told her how much I loved her and she replied 'I love you too mum'. The words will stay ever in my heart. Thank You Baba. Christmas was a non-event for me particularly when the family ignores Baba, but my daughter said She Loves Me.

Kala and Henry paid a visit bringing me many gifts from PN, having just returned from their holiday, especially the beautiful pictures of Swami's Lotus Feet and my Shirdi Baba's picture.

27 December

Radha and his two girls took me to see *The Flame* in Hurstville. This was a flame, which had been materialised by Swami in a house. We attended bhajans, and then were allowed to take water from where the lingam was immersed and *The Flame* was kept in front of a photo of Swami. We then went to Roberto, Theresa and Gorvina's lavish home where we saw the Swami Mini Mandir with Swami's jhoola made by Theresa, photos, and the place where *The Flame* is housed. Then we went into the lavish house and the *room* where it first appeared. There were two gowns on a bed presented to this family by Swami. I had to touch them. Radha and I were in our element at all Theresa's stories and experiences of Swami. They are truly blessed by Swami. I can't wait for her book to come out. I was shown a japamala materialised for her by Swami and spent two glorious hours in Swami's presence. I even smelt vibhuti strongly many times. Before leaving, I was given two cuttings from Swami's robe by Theresa, (one for me and one for Di)—two pictures of *The Flame* blessed by Swami and vibhuti. I received the warmest hug from Theresa on leaving, saw also the most beautiful picture of Jesus materialised by Swami for this family. On 31 December, I had bhajans here to bring in 1999 with our beloved Babas. On 1 January, I spent the whole day talking to the Babas. Over the next twenty-three days, I received a number of confirmations of Baba's presence, a third piece of robe was left on my dining table at the New Year's eve bhajan. There were nine Indian mynah birds sitting together on the fence outside our home, looking in, and there was strong smell of vibhuti flowing right through the house, many times. There were two pieces of orange thread found near Swami's picture and every picture on the altar in my prayer room was shining with Divine Light, in particular that of my Shirdi Baba. Prior to all these leelas occurring, I had jokingly requested our co-ordinator to bring back a robe from Swami on His return. Swami did not send me a robe but a piece of it left by Swami Himself was more than sufficient.

I had left the unframed picture of Shirdi on the bed so that He could stretch His long legs and have a good rest. At aarti, this morning, Swami's picture holding the Shiva lingam turned into various hues of red and white, with Swami's hair and face changing, the eyes staring at me and ripples of colour going through the hand and face. I was awestruck. It lasted for about five minutes and I thank You Swami.

1999

January

2 January

Happy happy new 1999. May the Babas bless, protect and love us all. Bhajans went well. Just now at noon aarti, Baba gave me a beautiful though brief darshan from some of the pictures. May the Divine Light of Shirdi Sai Baba, Sathya Sai Baba and Jesus Sai ever shine in my life. My friend Alika visited and witnessed the life-like image of Shirdi Baba on the wall and called it a very spiritual corner.

I received a beautiful darshan from 'the corner'; it was like Shirdi Baba was 'smoking bubbles'. Thank You, even though it was brief. My Baba is my life, my life is my Baba.

10 January

First bhajan for the year at our Centre was held. I was very happy to attend. Even in the Study Circle, we were all at our arguing best. Swami must be chuckling. Before I left for bhajans, I was waiting for Kala and Henry and noticed a piece of orange thread near Swami's picture at the entrance to our home. It is the size of a cotton piece from the two little bits I have in the purse. I felt again that Swami is saying that He had placed it there.

****

Mr Lodhia, my dentist's father was cremated today. After the cremation I tried to make my friends Henry, Kala and Raj laugh. It was a long, hot day and I said to Henry and so did Raj that we were very hungry and perhaps we should go to McDonalds to eat. I deliberately stated McDonalds as they are strict vegetarians, especially Henry, but I was hoping he would see the humour in my statement. Henry threatened to leave me at Leppington Cemetary, but we did end up at McDonalds, Henry ate chips only. While we were at Lodhia's, Ashok, his son, was performing all the Hindu death rituals. It was a sweltering day, about 40 degrees, when suddenly there was a massive gust of wind. Every window and door in the house shut loudly and then opened again. There were no fans on. It only lasted a second, but my feeling was that Mr Lodhia's soul had just been released. Baba bless him. Quite awesome!

13 January

Early this morning, I saw a large frame that looked like a collage of Swami, with His hands, etc., all moving very quickly. I stared at this moving picture, but could not decipher the words uttered or the actions. Then I moved away and muttered to myself, 'I better ring the airline to book my ticket to PN '. Next I saw some antiquated planes all around. The dream ended.

Swami, am I being summoned to PN? Hope so. I do long to go back.

18 January

My bathroom was filled with the smell of camphor; thanks Baba.

21 January

Excerpt from *The Touch of Baba* by Joyce Darlene Barker
  Be what you profess to be
  Speak what you intend to do
  Utter what you have experienced
  No more no less   Sathya Sai Baba

22 January

I did Samaritans last night (fifteen calls), one in particular was very interesting. A young Indian guy from Serampore, Calcutta, rang to say that they were about to end their marriage and after listening to both parties, I was getting nowhere with advice. I changed the subject and spoke of Swami, well, I got a surprise when he mentioned to me that he was one of the architects/designer of the Super Speciality hospital in Puttaparthi. Though he was not a Swami follower (however, he mentioned that most of his friends were), I indicated to him that Swami had sent him to me. Swami I place this at Your Lotus Feet, please give him and his wife some sense, I couldn't.

Darshan and Thread Story

As I was hyperactive this morning, I decided to clean and vacuum the house. After dusting Baba's picture and vacuuming the area where I found the orange thread on 2 January, I saw another piece lying there. I immediately said to Swami, 'if *You* have put this second piece here please give me a sign *soon*'. An hour later I did the noon aarti. Lo and behold, I saw Baba's Divine Light. Shirdi Baba on the wall was gently moving, (sometimes He does and sometimes He blows some smoke at me – [from His chillum!!]). Shirdi Baba's picture 'came to life'. This is the simplest way I can describe Baba's beautiful answer, darshan and leela. Thanks for the answer so soon Baba.

26 January

In my dream, I saw myself baby-sitting a very *thin* Indian child with a 'pageboy' haircut. He was meant to be a baby but turned into a toddler who followed me everywhere. I was trying my best to take good care of the child and carrying him around. I was also talking to him saying, 'we must cut your hair so that you will look like a boy'. There appeared to be an Indian festival being celebrated with lots of 'Indian happenings' around. I was surprised to see Henry in the crowd lighting up a cigarette. As usual, I made a comment to him and he put it out. Then I saw myself still holding the child, pointing to a picture of Baba and saying, 'See Baba, Baba'. The picture then became covered with vibhuti, which delighted me, so I touched the picture and blessed us with the vibhuti. The dream ended.

February

House Bhajan (4 February)

During bhajans here we had a cosy crowd. Thanks for Kala's help everything was organised but in our 'chit-chat session' about Raj and her new fiancee, I forgot to put out the Lotus Feet of Swami. After everyone left, Rohit explained very beautifully to me about Shirdi Baba's *mandorla*,(a picture of Shirdi Sai with words written in some Indian dialect, I think it is Marathi) and then Henry, Kala and I retired exhausted but happy at about 10.00 p.m. I was lying in bed contemplative about the evening, when I heard the most beautiful music coming from the altar area. I know I had turned off the bhajans, but this was ever so beautiful and was definitely not coming from my neighbour's residence. It lasted about three minutes, then stopped. I knew it was the Babas. I was happy with the bhajan.

This morning at aarti, I asked Baba, 'Was that *You* playing that glorious music last night, if so, please give me a sign'. On my way to work I saw the biggest, brightest rainbow, then another, a dual rainbow. Oh the bliss of seeing and hearing God's presence.

At aarti, the beloved's face *glowed*. I experienced 'puffs of smoke being blown into my face' (the chillum is being smoked by Shirdi Baba while His image on the wall waved and moved). My beloved Baba I love You, Your compassion and kindness. May Your Divine Light ever shine in this home and in this heart.

A Strange Dream (10 February)

I awoke from it at 1.30 a.m. In my dream, I was looking at a statue of Our Lady. I touched the statue and it came to life. Our Lady was talking to me and telling me about Armageddon. I kept trying to hold Her hand and ask for Her blessings. The next day was very dark, the sun was shining no more but appeared to be falling to earth. Everyone looked very scared and in a panic. I was terrified and full of anxiety for Lisa, who was in school. I kept trying to ring the school but could not get through. I kept repeating Our Lady's name to keep Lisa safe and bring her home safely. I was crying and very sad. I then awoke and in fear kept the bedroom light on all night. What does this strange dream hold for Lisa and Me? *Sai Ram.*

11 February

In my dream I saw a strange looking man with very *big eyes*. We were talking about Baba and I was ever so eager and willing to tell him about my Baba and me. He was interested in Baba but not in my conversation. I then looked around and saw Lisa as a little girl, happily playing. When I went to get her to go home or leave, she ran and disappeared. I kept looking for her anxiously, as she was lost. I awoke.

12 February

I was in a tall building where there was an earthquake. We got out safely but into a huge mudslide—again got out safely but my concern was for Lisa. Also, I saw myself attending a friend, giving him medication as he had a headache. Eventually, after getting into taxis, buses, etc., to get away from the dirty mud to safety, to Lisa, I found a phone and managed to ring Lisa. I heard her voice saying they were all safe. I was happy and awoke. The dream ended. I may mention here that when my daughter Lisa was born, I dedicated her to Our Lady, and I still pray to Our Lady to look after Lisa. The three dreams mentioned earlier seem to be connected.

Mahashivaratri—Valentine's Day (14 February)
I went to Penrith with Kala, Henry and John for bhajans being held there. The bhajans were beautiful and Henry outdid himself singing so well. It was extremely hot and I was being bitten by mosquitos. Rohit worked like a Trojan and Radha moved the fan away from me. Flower fell from Swami's chair when a child sang.

My Funny Valentine
A month before this day I kept pestering Baba, as I often do, 'Baba, Valentine's day is coming, can I expect to receive Red Roses from You?' As the day approached I retired for the night still loving Baba all the same, even though I did not receive any roses from Him. The next morning I had to go to the Post Office to buy a book of stamps. When the lady at the counter presented the book to me, I burst into laughter, the print/book of stamps were all *red roses*. Better late than never, He did give me my red roses in stamp form. I love You so Baba. Happy Valentine's day.

Baba's Humour (28 February)
I was listening to some jazz on radio 2CCR FM (I know Baba liked Jazz too so did Swami). I made a quiet comment to myself, 'nice if they could play some Nat King Cole on the radio Baba!' Guess what! Nat just sang 'Route 66'. Thank You Baba, You must like him too.

Thank You beloved Baba for shining Thy Divine Light at noon aarti today, let Thy Will be done.

In my dream it was early morning in India and Rita was serving food. She handed me a thali of rice. I asked her for only a small portion of parantha and some dal. Then I saw her sprinkle some ash from the aarti plate. I was then standing near Shirin and could see Henry at some distance going towards the temple. I asked Shirin to take me into the temple so that I could see Shirdi Baba's silver statue. The dream ended here.

March

10 March

At aarti I spoke aloud, requesting a leela. It happened (in time too, Baba) and yes, I am being bold here but not rude. Just before arriving at work I saw the jet steam—Swami's affirmation to me that He had heard me and so His presence was seen by me. I saw the jet smoke three times today which really made my day. Thanks Swami. (Reader please note here, whenever I see a jet/plane flying over with steam pouring out, it is an affirmation that Swami is with me. This has been going on since Swami came into my life, when I requested Him during my first visit to Parthy, 'Swami, whenever I see a jet steam, I know it is You, wherever and whenever'. Likewise with Shirdi Sai, I have always stated, 'Whenever I have seen any number be it the number plate on a car or any other number that adds up to a nine, I know You are with me'. I have continued with this ever since.)

Baba's Leela (12 March)

On the way back home after work, the sky darkened, a very threatening storm was in sight. I freeze in fear when I see a storm and don't like being caught in one. I prayed all the way from work to home, 'Baba please no storm till we get home'. Happily, I got home safely and the storm was a mere storm in a teacup—it passed over peacefully. He even calmed the storms for me!

20 March

After feeling like 'the dark night of the soul' the day before, I was very happy to have seen my beloved's Divine Light shine forth at japa at morning. This beautiful appearance had absolutely lifted my low spirits. I go into a state of depression from time to time and depend entirely on udhi/vibhuti, and use no medications at all for any ailments that I have.

21 March

I kept on getting the smell of incense for most of yesterday only to realise it was the Shirdi incense I had burned at noon, but it pervaded the house very strongly at times late into the night. Thus Baba made His presence felt even though the incense had long ceased burning. I did not attend bhajans today I chose instead to worship at home. Glad I did. I was rewarded with an absolutely beautiful darshan from the Baba pictures in the lounge while doing japa.

April

10 April

Thank You Baba for sending an honest, sweet plumber like Karl to fix the water heater, which ended up costing $110 instead of $1100. At noon aarti I was very happy indeed to see Shirdi on the wall become very active. I knew there was a message coming through, but had to be more attentive. I love You Baba. After lunch I burped, thanked Baba and told Him I enjoyed the food.

12 April

I saw the white cloud today hovering all over the bedroom. At times it was quite thick, it just drifted in and around and I just watched till it disappeared. I wonder what it is.

The answer just came to me. I just finished my prayers and realised that before I slept last night, I asked Baba, 'If that is Your soul or spirit on the wall, please give me a sign or a dream tonight'. I never got the dream but the 'flying cloud' was my sign from Baba—my sweet darling Shirdi Baba—it was Him off the wall and airing His wings.

21 April

I was awake from 12.30 last night, just could not go to sleep, meditated for about fifteen minutes at 3.00 a.m., then eventually fell asleep at about 4.30 chanting 'I am peaceful'. I had a very peaceful and beautiful dream where I saw myself in a temple preparing for aarti, putting all the statues up; one fell down but I picked it up. I heard bhajans being sung outside the temple, saw Rohit come in. After really praying and meditating, I looked up to see the most beautiful picture of a very calm sea, with the moon shining on it ever so serenely. The whole scene was blissful and even though I had an awful night, I awoke in peaceful and blissful mood. *Sai Ram.*

May

1 May

I had a beautiful darshan at japa this morning. The Light shone bright and there appeared a purple aura/mist all around the picture. I felt so blissful, as if I was in heaven. Joy, joy, joy! I went to the Festival of Mind, Body and Spirit with Mum—a big disappointment—as the *Hari Krishnas* were not there and everything was so expensive. But surprisingly, I saw a stall with Swami Tours, and Swami's picture was been given by one of the stall holder. Further on, I saw Sathya Sai Book Stall. I ended up buying *More Cutting the Ties* by Phyllis Krystal and $20 ripped off. I also got a new book list. I was happy to see a Swami devotee, though I was not happy with the prices of the Sai books being sold, after comparing the prices with the ones sold in Parthy for a pittance. *Sai Ram.*

Leelas (3 May)

I had a do-list and needed to do some grocery shopping. I wanted to buy many things but only had $157.

****

In the train from Leumeah to Campbelltown, I saw a very beautiful cloud shaped like the Holy face of Jesus with His arms outstretched. Bliss!

I completed my shopping. Shopping and taxi back home came to exactly $157. The Babas helped with the shopping, so we did not go above budget.

Signs (13 May)

I had a great longing to go to Shirdi and PN; Puttaparthi again, if only Baba allows me to. The crying had started and the *urge* was sincere, I longed for my Baba at Shirdi, to revisit His Samadhi and get it right this time, to get everything from my Everything (if I am deserving), but let Baba's Will be done. The urge had become a longing. I asked Baba should I go to PN/Shirdi, please give me a sign. As I thought this while walking to Leumeah station, I looked up at the blue sky and saw a jet, the first sign. I got into the train and read the word 'sure' on the seat in front of me (second sign). I then waited with shradha (faith) and saburi (patience) to make my travel arrangements.

15 May

Around 3.30/4.00 a.m. I hugged *Sai Satcharita*. I had a dream. I saw Swami in His orange robe and bushy hair sitting and walking around a room where my nana (deceased) was looking at Swami puzzled. Mum was trying to ignore Swami; Jeff, Cheryl, a little child and others were observing, as was I hoping, praying and longing Swami to come to me as He had a plate of orange laddoos and jalebies on the plate and was giving them to all who wanted the same. Cheryl did. Jeff as usual was sniggering, but Swami spoke to him, after I thought I was going to be ignored. Swami offered the plate to me. I did not want to be greedy, so I took half a thick jalebi. Thank You Swami. I cannot recall Swami's words to me, for He did say a few. Then I saw Swami relaxing in a reclining position on the floor with the crowd still around him, but He was wearing beige pants and white shirt, which I had seen Him wear in another dream some months ago. We all heard a man selling sweets and Swami lifted His hand with a coin in it indicating what sweet He wanted. I asked Swami what it was and He told me the ingredients but could not recall the same. As I was getting upset that Swami had *to buy* the sweets, so I went outside to look for the sweetman but he had gone. My dream ended.

Thank You Swami for Your darshan, dream and jalebi and a piece of orange thread found on my bathrobe this morning which was lying on the bed. Now I know where and from whom they were coming.

Dream (31 May)

I had a very odd dream at about 4.30 a.m. First, I saw a man peeking in through a window. My curiosity was aroused and on questioning him as to what it was he was looking at he replied 'Shiva Lingam'. I did myself see a few small oval-shaped objects on the stands in the room but I moved on. Then I saw myself in another room seated alongside a lady who was looking at an album. She pointed to a picture in it and said to me, 'You look like the picture'. When I looked at the same it was Swami's picture. The lady then turned into Swami. Swami seemed rather large wearing a white gown sitting very comfortably in His usual way and gesticulating with His hands. I was very excited as we conversed and I kept touching and kissing the Lotus Feet. We had a long conversation, one of my questions being – 'Swami – my job?' Swami replied, 'You are working with adolescents, leave and you won't be working again'. I replied, 'But Swami I have to work'. Swami got up and went away. Then I looked at myself in a mirror. My hair looked like Lord Shiva's and I was wearing a bindi. Then I saw myself lost in the rain looking for the hospital, I could hear voices of boys talking in Hindi about Swami. My dream came to an end. I awoke.

June

5 June

I had gone to Perth WA, for my niece's wedding. Walking along a Perth city street, I stopped in sheer surprise and joy when we came upon a shop called 'Sathya Sai Oasis'. It was empty. They had moved to a new location, but my prayer to Swami the previous night was answered. He showed me that He was with me.

7 June

The hills are beautiful, serene and so is Ali, a Swami devotee, who has kindly allowed me to stay with her here in WA. On meeting her I burst into tears. She is a woman of substance, so warm and welcoming to a stranger. I loved her instantly, her home and her garden. After lunch we went for a drive then to a great tea house which looked akin to a dungeon and ate the best Devonshire tea. Then we came back home and chatted about our beloved Swami. There was so much to say about Him!

10 June

I went to Perth city—fabulous cafes! I Got to 'Sai Oasis'. I loved the whole concept of it. The library, the puja rooms, meditation area and *The Babas*. I wanted so much to take home the picture of my Shirdi but there was no sale. Ali and I did some seva—we minded the store while Winnie, the little Jewish owner from Burma, sorted out some problems regarding the telephone, etc. I met Fiona, a lady who came in off the street to purchase a book on Swami. She told me about her having cancer and being cured by Swami and mentioned about the two books she had written. Ali and I then had coffee and biscuits and went to the Perth mint, where I bought the *last* small medallion of Swami. I rushed home to get ready for bhajans at Thornleigh. I was shocked on entering the puja room at Thornleigh. Every picture was covered in vibhuti, water was coming out from a rock, sugar from Shirdi Baba's beard, kumkum on all the statues, Ganesh was sitting in a bowl of amrit, Swami's entire chair was covered in vibhuti, kumkum and chandan. This was in Perth, Western Australia.

After bhajans, Nirmala, a lady who takes the form apparently of Shirdi Sai, did not change into Shirdi but she did say God bless you to me, when I walked past her (earlier at bhajans I had asked Shirdi Baba to bless me). The daughter very sweetly told me a few stories on the materialisations and gave me four containers of vibhuti, amrit, water and sugar to take back to Sydney.

I was very sad to be leaving Ali, a lady who had taught me much in the four days that I had been with her. Thank you Ali. Before the flight took off, I was looking out of the window, praying that there be no turbulence and the journey would be smooth. I noticed the most clear and beautiful rainbow, not in the sky but pouring onto the grass, one end was in the sky the other end just the colour of gold, pouring onto the grass. I have never seen anything so beautiful in my life, God's very own self. I was so blissful, I cried to see such pure beauty, a rainbow not in heaven but on earth.

July

Dream (5 July)

I saw myself in a compound. Two men on the side said *Sai Ram* and I responded excitedly, telling them I was a Sai devotee. They passed by me and put lots of vibhuti on my forehead and left a packet of vibhuti which I took. They went away and I approached the gate of the compound, where I was happy to see Baba standing. I went to touch Him, He looked very angry with me, frowning in fact and brushed off my hand, I shrugged and said, 'Okay Baba, be like that ignore me'. I guess Baba does not want me at Shirdi or PN, maybe I should become quiet and humble. There was the strong and beautiful fragrance of vibhuti.

8 July

I finished reading *Life History of Shirdi Sai Baba*. *Koti koti pranaams* to my beloved. At lunch returning to work I was delighted to see an *orange* car parked outside the hospital, with a number plate 'SAI'. Oh what bliss! I had also experienced the wonderful aroma of vibhuti. I have to ask here who is the driver of this car? I hope I get to know and see.

12 July

I had a beautiful vision at afternoon aarti. I saw the four *panatis* (lights) burning of Shirdi Baba with the brick in the middle with my beloved Shirdi in His zari shawl saying *Aao* – Come to Me. I pray this is Baba's consent for the trip.

16 July

At work today a patient in a wheelchair started talking to me about yoga at clinic this morning. She does it twice a week. She then started telling me a story about someone giving her ash which she used to put on her legs, and she had no more of the ash left. I was joyous inwardly and took the opportunity to tell her about Swami and vibhuti. She listened to my stories and asked me for some vibhuti. I was very happy indeed to accommodate her desire by giving her vibhuti. The conversation was getting even more exciting, as it is wont to do when speaking of Swami, when she had to leave. Ah! the ups and downs of life!

17 July

A few months ago, while I was praying in the puja room at home, I noticed a white manifestation on a part of the brick wall that lay behind the main altar. I looked and looked only to come to the discovery that it was actually Shirdi Baba in His white kafni, sitting with His legs crossed as He does in a lot of His pictures. I saw Him very clearly and even asked Him if this was Him in that form, to which I have had many signs of His sitting there. There is only one other of my friends who had recognised Baba in this pose, but to this day, and I pray I will forevermore, know and see Him on the wall every day. Other people have seen Ganesha in that corner and another lady once mentioned that although she saw nothing in that corner she felt it as being extremely spiritual. Reference is made to Shirdi on the wall many times in the book.

20 July

Thank You, thank You, thank You my Babas. The wonderful word 'Travel' was etched on a seat before me on the way home from work on the train again. Your approval was gratefully received and appreciated. I shall now put the travel plans into action, seeing that *Thou doest want me to go to India.*

25 July

Interesting Study Circle, i.e., *seva*. I was happy to have served the plants and pets well, even if human beings came third on the list of my seva. At afternoon japa, after a few weeks now, I noticed a very faint light on the picture. Divine Light was emanating from Shirdi Baba's picture, but even fainter from Swami. I was happy all the same for Your Divine Mercy towards me. I promised to buy Shirdi Baba a chillum or two when I would be in Shirdi.

Baba's Leela for Today (30 July)

The smell of vibhuti was so strong, that I felt as if it was glued into my nose. It also kept coming and going. Every time I read about my beloved Shirdi I wanted to cry. I had a lot of travelling ahead. I could not decide and placed the following options at Baba's Feet. I chose to pick out the answers like Shama used to do in the *Sai Satcharita* —*(a)* fly Qantas; *(b)* spend two nights in Shirdi; *(c)* and another four weeks to leave for the journey. I surrender to Thee completely Baba.

August

Started Shirdi Saptaha (5 August)

I kept getting very strong smells of vibhuti, especially at work. At times it was so strong, I felt like Baba was right there at work with me.

13 August

I got an eyelash in my eye and could not take it out. I asked Baba to help me and remove it for me. He obliged, it was removed in a second, thank You Baba, I need You for everything, my everything. It usually takes me much drama and trauma before I can get the same out. Also thank You Baba for letting me thread the needle at first go. This 'event' if unaided by Baba, takes about fifteen minutes before the eye is found on the needle, even though I wear my glasses while doing this. With Baba's help it gets done on the first go. Thank You Baba, for being my handyman too.

Oh How I Love Thee Baba, I Cannot Count the Ways (16 August)

After a few days and nights at last, the Divine Light shone on *bechara* (me). Deep in my heart I knew my Baba was removing the darkness and letting me into *Thy Light. Koti Koti pranaams Baba.* Must be my lucky day. After work, just before opening the front door, there was the most fragrant smell of jasmine vibhuti. And no, we did not have any jasmine growing around there either!

Leela (19 August)
I wanted to say '*Sai Sai Sai*' 900 times today. I said a quick prayer to Baba that when I reached the 900th Sai, please give me a sign that I have done so. I was merrily photocopying some work when I got the *strongest* smell of camphor for about a minute. *Koti koti pranaams Baba.* Thank You for Your joy.

Dream (22 August)
Before I went to bed last night I expressed to Baba 'please let me have a dream of Thee'. I did, even though it was a short one. I saw, as usual, a large crowd and at the far end was Swami, perched mid air on a chair, in a white gown, waving and blessing the crowd. I wanted to get closer to Swami so ran towards a line, only to be last in the line, and on getting there, found that Swami had gone into the mandir. My dream ended. I was disappointed on waking up nonetheless, but prayed that I got the first position and not the last one in the line.

Big Leela (24 August)
I got a receipt from, Shirdi Sansthan for the donation I had sent. I never expected or wanted a receipt. Thank you kind folks of Shirdi! Best of all though that enclosed with the receipt was a packet of udhi and sugar. It felt like receiving a gift straight from Shirdi Baba Himself. Thank You my sweet, beloved Baba.

30 August
Baba is so sweet. I did not have too much to do at work today, so was getting a little anxious. I looked at Shirdi Baba's picture on the computer and said 'we need some more work, we have run out'. Kirsty, the audiologist sought my help with a howling baby, who was sobbing and was in much distress, and had been crying continuously for half an hour, making it impossible for her to do the audiology test on the baby. I carried the baby and quietly chanted '*Om Namah Shivaya*' (today being Monday—Lord Shiva's day). The baby quietened down with me continuing to carry her, peacefully

asleep and the test was carried out this way. Thank You Baba for such a beautiful leela, for the seva done, and for a quiet time well spent.

September

Shirdi/Prashanti Nilayam (6 September)

I was flying to Mumbai via Bangalore by Air India. Baba was travelling with me. The Qantas part went with no problems of weather, etc., but thereafter, there was a terrible storm. The turbulence was scary. I kept repeating Baba's name, He never failed me, He kept me calm. I had a bad nose bleed with clots. I put vibhuti on it and the bleeding stopped. We stopped at Bangalore to drop off passengers and then took off for Mumbai. I have been on the plane from 12.30 p.m. on 6 September to 4.30 a.m. the next day. I met an interesting fellow sitting beside me, on the way to Mumbai. He read my palm but I was a bit put off when he started indulging in the whisky at that hour of the morning. From Mumbai we drove straight to Shirdi where the driver went round in circles and we only got to the magnificent place, 'The Sun-n-Sand' at 11.30 a.m. I was very tired but I indulged in a channa batura and lassi, and decided to tour and pray the next day. I was surprised when a complimentary basket of fruit and biscuits was sent by the General Manager. My Baba does love me as I do Him so very much. There was a beautiful painting of Baba in the room which I wished to take home.

Shirdi Village (8 September)

We slept well till around 12, and then stayed up for most of the night. I had fever but I was fine now. I went to my beloved Shirdi Baba's Samadhi. Before getting there this fellow tagged on (a guide sent by Baba). He took us to all the right places. Everything in the village had now changed and I was so happy to be there with my beloved. I visited Dwarakamai, Gurusthan, Chavadi, Samadhi mandir where a kind gentleman explained to me about the queues. For some unknown reason I was taken to the side of the mandir and did not have to stand in queue (we all knew why this was, if not for His Grace). I made the offerings and received the prasad. I toured the whole complex 'barefooted'. My only sadness was the hurriedness caused by the myriads of visitors who all love Baba. Hence, one could not stand in one place long enough to offer one's thoughts and prayers when one has to constantly move along. But my love for Baba was in my heart and I was ever so grateful to my Baba for me being at His beloved Lotus Feet at Shirdi once again. Next, I went to the village to feed the poor. It was gratifying and humbling. I will never forget it and prayed that Baba sent me back there soon to do the same. Then I visited a school where I met the Principal and two teachers. They were very happy to receive the books, toys, biscuits, etc. The Principal made the kids queue. One little lad had to play a big drum and all waved and said 'Thank You'. I was moved. Thereafter, I went to Kopargaon and visited a few beautiful temples including the Mahalakshmi Temple. I also went to Shirdi Baba's good devotee and friend Abdul Baba's Masjid and Samadhi, which was a very big place. Further down I went into the village to buy my Baba His chillum as I promised Him I would; I bought Him three. I came back to 'Sun-n-Sand'. Baba permitting, I would have liked to purchase the painting of my Baba in the room. Talking about VIP treatment, on entering my room after worship there was another basket of fruit for me. Thank You Baba. Lunch was great, puri bhaji with shrikhand (thought shrikhand was some sort of salad; it was pure sugared cream, delicious even though rich, especially eaten with gulab jamuns)—five puris (Baba ate nothing), potato *bhaji*, yummy salad, lime juice, pickles (wished I had a bottle to take home), gulab jamuns all for $8 only. A veritable *feast*. I slept the whole of the afternoon and well into the night. It was now 4 a.m., and I was contemplating as to how to transport Baba's painting to Sydney. *Sai Ram.* I placed that at His Lotus Feet (having begged the hotel manager to allow me to buy the painting and after much persuasion on my part and anger on his, he consented and allowed me to buy it). I hoped they packed it well and light. I fancied Baba travelling around as my travelmate. I thanked Baba for everything. I loved Him and Shirdi, and prayed that He would please bring me back to Shirdi soon.

Shirdi to Mumbai (9 September)

I fed the poor once more. I had a long, hot, smelly, wet journey to Mumbai. I left Shirdi at 9.45 a.m. but the traffic was being held up by an accident, and only arrived in Mumbai at 5.00 p.m. I didn't like Mumbai and the hotel I boarded. I should have spent another day in Shirdi not in this Shylock's Den. This was an unnecessarily expensive and unfulfilling place to be. I was complaining to Baba at the comparison in prices and services between here and Shirdi. Shirdi is the best place on earth to be. *Sai Ram.*

10–11 September

After checking out we went to the Bank, the ATMs give you cash but no balances. Then I went to the Mahatma Gandhi Museum, a really interesting place. Then on to my dearly beloved's mandir. I was very happy. I got delicious prasad from one and even managed a light *padanamaskar* on one of the statues of Shirdi Baba. It was fun to enter the mandir, in the slush, I felt very humbled and happy and my intensity of love for my beloved Baba was so very sincere that sometimes I felt my heart would explode with my deep and pure love for my Baba. I didn't feel sad any more, just very glad to feel so much love for Baba. I got caught in heavy traffic for four hours. There was heavy rain and I was rushing to get to the jeweller by 8.30 p.m. Then I was on to Tiffany's with the driver for masala dosa and nimboo pani. I was honoured to dine with the driver. He was a good boy, and was very shy to share the table with me. I rushed to the airport. The plane left on time and once again, the beloved Baba came to my assistance. I was a little anxious about placing the beloved's portrait on the plane, but surprisingly, we not only got a first class Air India flight, much better than the last plane, but my Baba and I were also given the last seat on the plane and there was plenty of storage place. Baba in His painting, had His own seat next to me. The journey was smooth and I thanked Baba for His Grace. I arrived half an hour late and was met by Clipper's driver Bul Bul, a very patient man, unlike me. Except for one minor incident, the trip was fine. I stopped at a village, I thought the driver was thirsty, so he went for tea while I sat in the car on the way to Parthy. The car was surrounded by the village boys who wanted pens, I only had one. So I gave it away. They all scattered admiring the lucky boy and his pen.

I reached Parthy at 6.30 a.m., and waited outside the gates of the Super Speciality Hospital of the Gupta family. The Seva Dal would not let us enter the hospital so I just sat in the car and waited. I met Dr Gupta briefly. He was a nice chap. He introduced me to another doctor who gave me a chit for PN and asked me to give it to the admitting officer. Unfortunately, there was no room at the Ashram. They offered me the sheds but I was not interested so just waited along with my Shirdi Baba (who has all the saburi in the world) till something became available. Four hours later a German lady approached me saying she had a spare bed in her room. I was very happy and stayed at N3-D18. Reader, please note the room number. It was very humid. I had the first darshan of Swami this afternoon but I was very tired and sleepy. I got row 6. Seeing Swami, I shed a few tears.

12 September

I was up for Omkara (splendid as usual). I got the seventh row. I was gradually getting back to my elements. I was happy to see our beloved Swami look so well. He had a joke with one of the devotees. I was very happy to hear Him speak. I had an excellent darshan. *Koti koti pranaams* Swami! I did not stay for bhajans, as the back was bad, the hunger was worse. After a hearty, too hearty breakfast, Gaby (the lady with whom I was sharing the room) led me to a side alley where we sat and waited till the end of bhajans and lo, Swami came out, on the way to his mandir. More tears were coming out of my eyes. Next, I went to a lecture given by Anil Kumar. I understood why he is Baba's interpreter. Besides being very suave, with a wonderful wit, he was an absorbing lecturer. During the afternoon darshan, I was in row twenty-three but had what an awesome darshan! Up, close and personal of the Swami kind. Though seated at the back, I had a perfect view of Swami and Swami stood at the altar a longer time than usual, in full view. The Italians had a very long interview. Gaby and I had a good satsang last night, so we did not get much sleep. Besides, it was very hot and we had mosquitoes in the room.

13 September

I woke up very early around 4 a.m. for darshan (Ganapati Chaturthi). I sat from 4.45 a.m. to 9 a.m. I had intense pain at the back and I had no energy. Swami gave a beautiful darshan. We got row twenty-seven, and my heart strings were pulling towards Shirdi again. I wanted to go back. I kept remembering the humbleness of Shirdi Baba and His meagre surroundings. I could not immerse myself at darshan, my buttocks was so sore, the mind was everywhere, and my heart was in Shirdi. I knew people say 'Sathya Sai is the reincarnation of Shirdi Sai', but I continue to see them as two separate beings, my Shirdi Sai and my Swami Sathya Sai.

Gaby said she felt a strong smell of something beautiful last night, but I was asleep. I missed again. Swami was magnetic and very charismatic. At afternoon discourse, the energy was very low as was the intellect. I got the tenth row. It was good to hear and see Swami in real life, My body and mind felt very tired. I felt that I didn't belong here and that I needed to go back to Shirdi. After the discourse, Swami sang beautifully. He did not like one of His bhajans, and showed His dislike of the same in the middle of a sentence and started a new bhajan. I chuckled. I was happy about the praise given to Lord Ganesha, I loved Him too.

Row 24 (15 September)

At darshan I sat against the wall, the mind was everywhere and the body felt worn out, but I had good darshan of Swami coming out of the mandir. Days and nights were very humid, more so without the fan, Gaby kept putting it off as she did not like it. I had to shut up and put up with the heat and mosquitoes. There was a big function in the afternoon with all the students bringing in pandals and floats of Lord Ganesha (apparently this is done every Ganesh Chaturthi here. Swami broke, after blessing them all, about twenty coconuts and laughed all the way while doing so. Gaby and I left as it was very loud, and walked up to the meditation tree for serenity. I meditated for about ten minutes then walked through a lovely garden constructed by a foreigner, with the statues of Buddha, Jesus Christ Ganesha, etc., and guess who I then spotted? It was my beloved Shirdi Sai. I hastened to Him and kissed His Lotus Feet. I was a bit sad that poor Shirdi Baba was roughly painted on a piece of rock and left to all the elements. There was not even a *chattar* (umbrella) over Him. I had to complain about this to Swami.

Row 21 (16 September)

Seva Dals left today, so I got excellent darshan. Swami meandered between them, took their letters and gave them prasad. Even though I was against the wall, I saw Swami very clearly; after blessing, Swami waved to all. After dinner, Gaby and I strolled to where the sheds were, I was thankful to Swami for not sending me there. Community living, not for me Swami!

Row 2 (17 September)

Swami took my letter today. He went past so fast that I had no time for a glimpse. A bit shy, I stood up all the same and put the letter out. Whoosh! it was taken. If only I were nearer so that the gown could have been touched or words whispered to me! Perhaps at the next visit. I was grateful though for the letter being taken by Swami. I also opened Shirdi Sai's painting to show Gaby, now I would have to pack it properly. Mentally I was very restless, my mind was filled up with endless questions. I didn't find it wrong in my heart to worship the two Babas separately, but then there were so many questions on that issue.

18 September
My questioning mind was again at work during darshan. Why was I there? Besides physically, I was not feeling too well; I thought I had 'flu'. After darshan, I spent some quiet and loving time in the garden with my Baba. I was approached by an Irish nurse asking if I could do some seva. My mind was still for the moment. I thought I needed to do some work. Gaby was happy now. Swami walked by her. I was off again to the garden to be with my Baba.

Leela
Swami's picture by the staircase, where our room was, had started materialising vibhuti. The Seva Dal explained to me that Swami often materialised vibhuti on the pictures. Thanks Swami, it was a lovely gesture.

Row 21 (20 September)
I had good darshan. I left soon thereafter as something was nagging at me to ring my mother in Australia. I was shocked, Kristian, my nephew, seemed to have a carcinoid on his lungs! I prayed to Baba/Swami/Jesus to help him and the family. He was only twenty-five years old.

Row 12 (23 September)
I got up at 4.30a.m. and was in line by 5 a.m., but the crowds were too much. Even though it was only 7.25 a.m., the heat was intense. I had a good darshan, in spite of the crowds, but left earlier due to the mob (I get claustrophobic in a crowded place). Gaby got the first line again and managed to touch the Lotus Feet. Me? I had to be grateful for even being here.

Dream
I did seva in the western canteen after breakfast, had a chuckle as I had never worn an apron before, but was very happy to do seva. I rushed to do bhajans just in time, and managed to get a glimpse of Swami. Then I spoke to a lovely Singaporean lady whose husband was very ill. I was visited by Sathya, the Italian lady, who lived in Prashanti. She asked me to do seva for Shakuntala the next day. She noticed the painting of Shirdi Baba and commented about the energy coming from the painting also about my closeness with Him. I loved Him so much. Perhaps we were connected in some way in the past, but how Baba, please enlighten me. Also she told me about a Shirdi temple between here and Bangalore where pujas were held for twenty-four hours. Thank You my Baba, I wouldn't wait to get there.

Row 11 (24 September)
I went early enough, but Swami when coming out of the mandir looked directly at me with a very *stern* look. Sathya, a devotee here, and I were discussing the poor state of the general hospital, lack of staff, saving of cotton balls, etc. She was a woman after my own heart. We felt that like the Super Speciality Hospital, the General Hospital too could have an uplift. Shakuntala, the patient we were looking after at the General Hospital, looked bright, clean and almost normal but for the cast on her leg. The mind was ever questioning. I prayed for some answers from Swami. I had made a vow to visit Shirdi, Baba was willing, for as long as and whenever God permitted me to I wished to feed the poor, even if it was for two days in a year at His Samadhi.

Row 26 (25 September)
What can I say, I was sitting up against the wall in the Sai Kulwant Hall, Swami coming in looked our way. I left after darshan to meet Dr Gupta and his family. I could not praise him highly enough, as he was so sweet. I went to their lovely home where his wife made delicious masala dosas for breakfast and tea, and showed me all their films with Swami. They were an extremely *blessed* family, the pictures showed Swami blessing the baby, naming her Saisemina, giving her a chain, clothes, the cradle, and there were many other pictures of Swami and Saisemina. The little girl was a delight and so were her parents. They showed me the emerald ring Swami

materialised for Saisemina, the medallion for his wife, diamond earrings and, the lingam for her (which Sunil put water over and allowed me to drink and wash with the water. I felt cleansed and blessed). I watched a video too of Swami and them. Then Sunil took me to the Super Speciality Hospital. Wow! Massive, clean and well-equipped. They have every modern facility here. Super indeed!

I had a very pleasant morning with a very dynamic couple who were truly blessed by Swami. I had just eaten three hot boiled eggs (courtesy Mrs Gupta) and a 'Ditto' Mango. I felt almost normal again and the sweet doctor also gave me tablets. How kind and hospitable was this family, who were to me complete strangers. With Swami's grace, Sunil gave me two packets of vibhuti, given to them by Swami. I felt happy again and the big dark clouds that were looming before had left me. On returning, I bought two garlands at the Ganesha gate. On visiting my beloved Shirdi stone in the garden, a man asked me if I put flowers there. I said, 'Yes'. He then took a flower from the garland and stuck it on Baba's forehead, it stayed. He then stated, 'He has accepted it'. I tried the same with much effort and falling at first, (saburi) it stuck. My beloved Baba, am I accepted by Thee?

After bhajans (which were great), I had a lovely chit-chat with my new friend. She was a wise lady and confided to me that her sister is the lady who ushers in all the interviewees at the altar. Such grace! Also she shared her address and shared some very private and sweet stories with me, i.e., the peaceful passing of her husband, etc. I prayed that we continue to be in touch for many more years. I visited the book store and bought three books—*Transformation of the Heart, Truth Is Only One,* and *The Greatest Adventure.*

Row 3 (26 September)

It rained all night, and I walked across puddles to have darshan; it was fun. Goodbye to Swami. I left Parthy today. It was 30 kms before Bangalore that we stopped at the new and very beautiful Shirdi Temple. The pujari did the puja and gave me a few things, but I was after the actual photograph of Shirdi Baba's Lotus Feet at the main altar. I prayed that I can be given the same by my Baba. Then I went to the Dhuni area and threw some logs in. I visited a beautiful pyramid-shaped temple surrounded by water, which contained another beautiful picture of my Baba and the 'Om' sign. It was so peaceful there. The pujari gave me vibhuti and prasad and a copper medal of Him, but I still liked to have the picture of the *Feet*.

28 September

My beloved Shirdi Baba's birthday—happy birthday to You my Baba. My prayer for this special day is that You take care of Kristian and make him well again. I went to the big Shirdi Temple in Cambridge Road. I was extremely lucky as the last aarti was on and they were to close at 12 noon. The gates were just about to be closed, the doorman must have seen the sad hopeless expression on my face so he let me go in. Baba had a big grin on His face, (I am sure it was because He saw me?) and though my time was limited with Him, I was given some prasad and some flowers which I was sure to take back, customs or no customs. Then I drove on to the three temples, 35 kms from Bangalore. It was raining, and I bought some prasad at the gate and got into the mandir where a puja was done for the whole family. I was also lucky enough to get all the bangles and things bought earlier. I touched the beloved Baba's feet.

I bought with my Baba's grace *Life History of Shirdi Sai Baba* and a larger picture of Baba, back to the Temple where I begged the pujari to give me the picture of the Feet of my Baba. After much begging, he sent the younger pujari to a nearby village in the pouring rain, and they gave me a beautiful big picture of my Shirdi Sai's Feet. It was pouring; I went briefly to the Dhuni mandir and threw two logs in, then to the Meditation mandir and laid a garland over my Baba's picture. I could jump puddles too, but only for Baba. I was not sad, I knew and felt my Baba in my heart and soul forevermore. I was drenched in rain but it was blissful. I was looking forward to buy sweets from KC Das for my Baba and me, in celebration of His birthday, but they were closed for lunch, though I was lucky to get a pineapple cake. So I sang Happy Birthday to my Baba.

29 September

It was midnight. I waited long at the Bangalore airport, which was full of mosquitos. I had to battle with them till 5.30 a.m., as we were an hour late. I got to Singapore at 11.00 a.m. and spent the day walking. I took off for Sydney on time (8.00 p.m.) and was happy that it was a refurbished plane and they placed my Baba (painting) in His own little cabin, safely. I did miss Him, not sitting next to me though. After an extremely smooth flight, no accidents or incidents, I arrived at Sydney around at 5.00 a.m., and got through customs easily enough without them even checking the wooden frame around the painting. I would like here to thank sincerely my beloved Shirdi Sai Baba and my beloved Sathya Sai Baba for their grace. May my life be ever filled with Thee and Thy blessings.

October

3 October
I believed my Shirdi on the wall was very happy with His new chillums. I did noon aarti and was joyous to see my beloved Shirdi 'cloud over' as if He was smoking the chillum and there was a lot of smoke around. Such a joyous darshan from Him!

Dream (4 October)
Koti koti pranaams my Baba. Before retiring for the night, I pleaded with Shirdi Baba that I would like to experience Him in His actual form. I had a dream where I could see pictures of Shirdi Baba everywhere and large crowds of people whereby I was telling them 'Worship Him, He is very powerful, He is alive and everywhere'. The dream ended. Thank You my beloved Baba for Your mighty darshan. May the experience of Your bliss, grace and blessings be ever with me and mine.

Dream (21 October)
Just a little dream but it made me happy. I saw myself amidst a large, very disorganised group of people, all trying to get a first row, to try and get a closer look at Swami. I was at the last row in a very dark room. I went outside on seeing a stall nearby. A little boy in the stall who looked like a *'young Sathya'* same hair and robe, approached me and asked me quietly if I knew of the child born in India. I replied, 'Yes, I knew Him, I knew Baba', very sharply. I then asked the boy if he was selling anything new on Baba as I had (ego) everything that was in the stall. I was rummaging but could find nothing new on Baba. This was the end of the dream, and I awoke.

November

Dream/Leela (4 November)
I had such a lovely dream between 4 a.m. and 5 a.m. I saw myself in a large field surrounded by flowers and Swami in a white robe was asking people the names of the flowers. I plucked one, and on turning around, Swami was standing right in front of me with a most beautiful bunch of fresh large daffodils and jonquils all facing me. Swami just put the large bunch in front of me, I touched the bunch and blessed myself after that. When I awoke I asked Swami for a sign that it was Him. I got it, on the way to work. I saw a *jet stream of smoke*. What a quick answer!

Akhanda Bhajans (14 November)
I went with Kala and Henry from 1 p.m. to 6 p.m. It was beautiful. I loved bhajans. *Reflections* was published in time for Baba's 74th Birthday. I was joyous to note that two stories one of John and the other by me too was published. *Sai Ram!*

28 November
Just before going to bhajans my 'back' had become stiff and was paining quite suddenly. It seemed to be moving away now. I heard lovely bhajans. I actually sang a few quietly. At noon aarti which I loved doing at home, I was very happy to see the reappearance of my Shirdi on the wall. I believe He was acknowledging the tobacco, *chappa* (cloth) to add to His chillum, and I did get Him the best tobacco, (Marlborough). I could see the smile on His beautiful face. He *shone* and so did I, it had been a long while since I last saw His Divine Light. I prayed, *keep it ever shining Baba.'* While I did not smoke myself, I indulged Baba from time to time with His chillums (as I know how He loves them). I write this in the present tense as these things *do occur* here, i.e., Baba smoking His chillum. I try to be ever mindful (when I am not forgetful, which is often), to remember that Baba *is ever here, and He is.*

December

2 December
Our beloved Nani (my mother's mother) passed away early this morning. May your soul be happy and peaceful our Nani, we all love you.

6 December

The funeral—what a lovely happy funeral! Even the priest Father McCormack, yes, the sweet priest who used to give me communion every day when I was ill with cancer, presided. We played 'I don't know why I love you but I do' one of Nani's favourite songs while we followed the bier into the chapel. *I love you Nani, may your soul be peaceful and joyful.*

18 December

Glorious day indeed! At noon aarti, brief but sweet and exhilarating all the same, the Divine Light shone on the mandir picture, a first from this picture. The three Devas (Jesus, Shirdi Sai and Sathya Sai) lit up and Baba on the wall glowed, brief, but wonderful all the same to see Thy Divine Light, as it always is.

31 December

At aarti this morning Baba made a 'brief' appearance by Light. I had a chat with Him. At noon aarti (truly blessed) my 'chat with Baba' from this morning was answered by Him. I got the most beautiful darshan of Baba. I realised something was about to happen when I saw the little statue of Shirdi Baba with the Light around it. The Lotus Feet on the big altar lit up, as well as the faces of Swami and Shirdi Baba. I was filled with the bliss, the grace, the joy, and love of my Babas.

2000

January

*Sai Ram and a Mirthful Millennium to All the World
(1 January)*
Bhajans went well at Rita and Radhas. I was humbled and grateful to do the aarti. I was even happier to have read *The Life History of Shirdi Sai Baba* at 3.00 a.m. A great and blessed way to start the millennium for me. *Sai Ram.* I spent most of the day watching the world in the new year brought together in such joy and happiness—the ABC had a brilliant 24-hour broadcast. I shed a few tears of utter joy to see the world as one in peace, even if it only lasted a night. May the peace of the Lord reign over all. *Sai Ram.*

Dream (5 January)
It was a very short and strange dream but I am grateful to Swami for His appearance, short though it was. People everywhere, saw Swami light something, I vaguely remember it being a bush. Swami was wearing a very beautiful golden gown. He then ascended and floated away. The dream ended.

15 January
I had dinner with friends at 'Woodlands'. Before leaving, I asked Baba if He would kindly escort me to dinner. I met a friend at the dinner who was wearing a beautiful chain and medallion with a big picture of Shirdi Baba wearing an orange kafni. Thank You my life long escort!

23 January
I went to bhajans, a bit upset—longing, yearning, craving, desiring to go back to Shirdi/PN. At meditation, I asked for a '*chota* (small) leela'. On the way back from bhajans, I saw Swami's jet steam. I read the whole book on *Shiva*. I loved it. At the end of the last

chapter, I got the smell of camphor which overtook the bedroom. I found many similarities between Shirdi Baba and Lord Shiva, i.e., chillum, dakshina, Reincarnation.

Thy Light (26 January)
Today is Australia Day and Indian Republic Day. Jai Hind. I awoke at 7.00 a.m. and did the usual chores and said a japa just before aarti. I would like to jump with joy but will stem my joy as I have begun to realise that every time I am elated it is immediately taken away from me and misery ensues. At the end of japa, Swami shone His Divine Light emanating from His face in the lounge, then the beloved Shirdi glowed. I continued to say another japa as I did not want to end this beautiful grace of the Babas. The grace continued. At noon aarti my Baba on the wall glowed. He appeared to be wearing a large garland around His neck, the conversation was one-sided, me only (Baba listened). He is so sweet. The small picture of Baba in the Temple also shone for just a second. I constantly chat with Shirdi Sai, sometimes even when I am praying. It is very spontaneous.

29 January
The most beautiful and first darshan from the painting of Shirdi Baba in the bedroom. After aarti, I was sitting and pouring out my problems yet once again to Shirdi Baba, when it first started in Baba's eyes; then the light went all over the beautiful face of my beloved Baba. I wanted to be overjoyed at this magnificent darshan from the painting but had to contain myself. At noon aarti, the lingam and the red picture of Shirdi Baba as well as the marbled picture in the Temple, shone the Divine Light. Joy, joy, joy! I forgot myself again. Is it not right to be so joyous on seeing God's divine glow?

February

Leela (3 February)
It was a very hot day. Train was cancelled. As I was leaving for work in my usual way, I reminded Baba once again with the words, 'I love You Baba, do You Love me' and I left for work. Finally, I was sitting in the heat on the station for half an hour, waiting for the next train. On approaching Ingleburn, I looked up at the clear beautiful blue sky to see a plane 'smoking a message'. Jesus, Jesus,

Jesus He loves you forever. I could not stop smiling; ask and you shall receive. Love you too Jesus and Baba, thanks for the immediate response. Oh how I love Thee, in every single way, and oh how You love me in all Your different forms.

Valentine's Day (14 February)

I have an allocated day off from work today (like to spend this day of love with Shirdi Sai Baba). After breakfast at aarti the darshan that Baba gave from His painting was to die for. I don't want to die now though, want to see more of this. I am lost for words – I will be Baba's instrument in writing this passage. I was expressing yet again to Baba how purely and sincerely I loved Him and wishing Him a Happy Valentine's Day from one who truly loves Him. I noticed a spark from the left eye of Baba, while His right eye opened and closed. The face started to glow and the effulgent divine light glowed from every area of the portrait, especially from the nose. This lasted for about 5-7 minutes. I was stunned. Thank You my beloved Valentine, I love You beyond eternity and what a Happy Valentine's Day it was! I didn't have to even remind You this year to buy me a present, You let Your Light shine on me.

28 February

Before sleeping last night, in my heart I prayed for a dream, even if it was short. After a harrowing night of nightmares, I saw myself at a computer searching the website. Baba appeared slowly. I looked very happy to see Baba on-line.

March

Mahashivaratri (4 March)

I went to Bonnyrigg for Mahashivaratri. I loved and enjoyed it. I got home at 10.30 p.m. and had to look in the mailbox as I was expecting my friend Alika to leave some papers in the mailbox, as I was out all day. On opening the mailbox, there was a letter there, on reading the same it was not from Alika as expected but from the Shirdi Sansthan with prasad and a receipt. I was baffled because this was a Saturday night and there is no mail delivered on Saturdays. I experienced even more joy as I discovered the three original pictures of Shirdi, Swami and Shiva that I thought I had lost, was found in the washing machine. Although they were given a good wash, I was able to recover them by drying them and putting them in my Sai Book. What a Shivaratri! *Om Namah Shiva Shiva Shivaya.*

5 March

At bhajans I bawled. The desire to go to PN and Shirdi was ever-increasing. But I could only leave this at Thy Lotus Feet, and it is Thy Will not mine. I was given some laddoo as prasad from Swami via Kala, (I must say thank you to Lord Ganapati for this, I did ask You for laddoos the other day), as well as an amazing picture of Shirdi Baba. The story of the picture being that Kala and Henry went to a school outside the Nilayam, while there was a person who gave Kala this picture of Baba. Apparently, the person and his wife went to the Samadhi of Shirdi Baba and took a picture of the same, but on development, the Samadhi didn't come out but the magnificent picture of my handsome Deva, Shirdi Baba. He looked a bit like Errol Flynn, the actor, in it. It had been a beautiful and meaningful Shivaratri. *Om Namah Shiva.*

Dream (14 March)

I saw myself in my dream entering a very beautiful bedroom, plush being the word. Someone told me it was Baba's bedroom. It had a lot of ornate wooden beams and pelmets, highly polished and a huge bed of oak wood with an exquisite green brocade and silk bedspread. I was in awe at such splendor and richness. I turned around to see Baba walking in, smiling and looking very happy and waving His hands. I then noticed this enormous *round* chair and was captivated by the silks and leather it contained. I was waiting to see Baba sit on it when I awoke.

Vibhuti Miracle—The Ant Story (18 March)

While I think ants are a pest at most times, especially when they are an invading army in one's house (I admire their resilience) especially when they never want to leave the kitchen, I try my utmost to avoid killing or hurting them when cleaning and cooking. I was baking a cake for my sister's birthday which was to be on the next day, the ants were busily doing their job as I was doing mine, and at the same time we were also trying not to get into each other's way. I was rubbing down the bench top before laying the ingredients, when I accidentally hurt one little ant. I saw the poor ant struggling to move and I was very saddened by his effort to stay alive and at my stupidity at hurting him. He tried unsuccessfully to move while I prayed to Baba to either let him die or live. It was a struggle for both of us. I went and got some vibhuti and spread it around the ant, before I could utter Baba, the ant was up and off like a shot, even crossing the vibhuti border. This leela was much appreciated Baba, I didn't bring the ant to life. You did, many thanks. I see You in most creatures great and small, therefore, even more so cannot and do not like to hurt You in Your varied appearances.

April

April Fool's Day (1 April)

Another ant story. Autumn is upon us and with it the ants start their hibernation (at least from the kitchens of houses of Sydney). I was thankful on clearing the kitchen this morning. No more little critters in my way, so no more mutilation of ants, which I really don't like doing, even accidentally. Sometimes the fault should lie with them too, they get in the way. I just about finished cleaning the last bench top when there to my despair Anty was swiped for a six by my dust-cloth. He lay there unconscious, smitten by my gloved hand. My heart melted, was he dead or just unconscious, another sin to be atoned for by me? I gave it a little nudge with the fingertip – no response. This calls for action, Baba's udhi/vibhuti to the rescue. I showered Anty with udhi, it seemed more like a burial than a revival. Again, before I could utter 'Sai' – up and risen and off was Anty! Well, doesn't this story make you really feel good. I can't stop smiling. But there's more, today is 1 April – April Fool's Day – now Baba, need I say more? I am not fooling you dear readers, but are the Babas fooling me?

Divine Light (9 April)

I did not attend bhajans today due to a sore throat – all that gossip at work, serves me right. I should learn to listen and remain speechless, but I have to speak the truth which people cannot stand to hear. At morning aarti, I received the sign from Baba which I had asked for during the week as to whether I should submit an application for the GM's office job. Shirdi Baba's eyes first closed gently, giving me an indication that He was present and watching. Then the face lit up and the Divine Light shone. I am learning to remain calm, I realise that when I become frantic with joy, bliss, etc., it always disappears almost immediately. I was serene. I am thankful to Baba for all the beautiful responses. I failed to mention earlier that my Baba on the wall *also glowed and moved*. I always know when He literally comes to life.

Dream (15 April)

In my dream, I was walking across a street and everywhere I went I found coins. I kept picking them up till my pockets bulged. Then I saw a fellow doing the same, so I stopped. I went into a book store and ordered volumes 1, 2, 3 and 4 of a Shirdi book. I noticed the girl packing volumes, 1,1,1,1 = 4. I told her I wanted volumes 1–4 not 1111. I awoke. I felt Shirdi Baba was saying something to me with the number 4 (4 vices). Four things that I must change. I will work it out and try to change when I do. This event did really occur in reality to me a few days ago. I was walking home from work. I went past the shops to notice a few gold coins lying on the grass. I naturally picked them up. A little further ahead there was another pile, I again picked up the same. I was now smiling at the unreality of this situation, not even remembering the dream about the coins I had a few days ago. Then I had almost reached home, when again there was another pile of gold coins. I picked these up too. Last but not the least and most surprising of all, when I was about to enter my house, there was another pile just near the stairs. I don't know what to make of this, except to say it is and will always be a mystery to me. Many people walk this route every day either to our local shops nearby or to the station. Surely someone would have noticed four distinct piles of gold coins lying on the road. I felt it was left there for me to pick up, the strangest one being at my very doorstep. There is a lot I do not understand in some experiences, but what does anyone really know of God and His ways.

17 April

Today is the 108th day of this millennium. We were to recite the Gayatri Mantra 108 times. I chanted the mantra at 6.30 a.m. before going to work. I started saying it in the puja room, then went all round the house to all the pictures and statues. I looked and looked again at the Buddha's statue in the lounge. The Divine Light was shining from Lord Buddha's face, the whole head was white instead of its normal dark colour. Then I saw the light coming from Shirdi Baba's and Swami's faces in the lounge. I felt very happy and blessed. Thank You my Baba/Swami/Lord Buddha.

Good Friday (21 April)
I cried all day, watched Our Lady of Fatima and Our Lady, Mother of Jesus. It was beautiful and I howled. I love You Jesus and our Holy Mother.

Leela (29 April)
I went for lunch with Mum (and Baba came too, I try not to forget to invite Him) and then to the Festival of Mind, Body and Spirit. I was surprised to see it less crowded this year, giving us room to move freely. There were fewer stalls and unfortunately no *Hari Krishna* food stall (the *Hari Krishna's* usually have a stall at the Festival, where they distribute delicious food samples to visitors there for free), but we enjoyed it all. The day was beautiful, especially the walk along Cockle Bay. I bought a T-shirt with Buddha on it and the words 'Mind Your Own Business'. I am taking it as a sign from Baba to me. Shall I try and heed these wise words? We also got a free bag. After coffee, I came home to find our bird not well at all. In fact, I thought she would fly off to Baba before nightfall. I was sad to see the pool of water surrounding her. Quickly, I poured vibhuti over her and prayed Baba to cure her, she is still too young to die.

30 April
All was well. The bird was back to normal, chirping as usual. Thank You Baba! At bhajans this morning and during meditation, I visualised Shirdi, Sathya and me together. We were talking, I was complaining, the Babas were listening. Then Shirdi Baba gave me a beautiful posy of gardenias (our favourite flower). After the discussions at the Study Circle was over, I helped in dismantling the altar and handing out the flowers, and asked all present there if they wanted any flowers. Kala took a rose and Prasanna told me to take the rest, a bunch of gardenias. I was overjoyed. Thank You for Your beautiful darshan Baba and Your bliss and the gardenias.

May

13 May
I went on a pilgrimage with Mum (and the Babas) today. We went to Penrose Park as it was the beatification of Francesco and Jacinta of Fatima after eighty nine years (two of the three children who saw are Lady of Fatima). We chartered a bus from Ingleburn and it took

about one and a half hours to get there. I was astounded at the place and the beauty of God surrounding it. On entering the Church I was very pleased to see the Monstrance open for all to see and it was like this for about an hour. There was a very large crowd of various dominations but the Portuguese were in abundance and did most of the flags, etc. The Church was very beautiful and simple and I was not only so joyous of seeing the Monstrance, but heard mass, received Holy Communion and said the rosary twice. I looked up at the sun to see it spiral and flowers like blue lotus spin in it. Mum saw people walk on the sun. We had a picnic lunch, then went to the Grotto for Benediction. I was in awe, when it was said in Latin. Latin masses are not held any longer. During the procession, Mum and I were close behind the Monstrance. It reminded me of school, and I felt very close to our Sweet Jesus at this stage. Our beautiful Lady of Fatima was carried on floats to the Grotto and I was happy that she is so revered by all. There were little girls all dressed in white throwing petals of roses along the way, and the sun shone like it was so happy, so was my heart. As the Monstrance and Our Lady were put down, we had a clear view of it all. I could see an aura or in my terminology of spirit, the Divine Light shine around Our Lady and very briefly though, round the Monstrance. I indeed was so pleased. Again I looked at Our Lady to see the same. After Benediction, which I again was happy to be at after many years, on our way back to the bus, I kept hoping that what I saw was the Aura indeed and not my imagination. My thoughts were confirmed when behind me I heard a tinkling of a bell. There was a beautiful serene priest, trying to make passage for him to pass as he was holding The Blessed Sacrament. I was very happy and felt full of grace at this Divine day. I love You Jesus, I trust You Jesus. I love You Our Holy Mother, I trust You Our Holy Mother. *Sai Ram.* May the Canonisation of our beloved Francesca and Jacinta be ever remembered. We got home at 6.30 p.m. after a very long but a day filled with Jesus' and His Holy Mother's grace.

19 May

Before leaving for work today, I asked Baba for some leela and something to write on the blank pages of the diary.

First Leela: On arriving at work, I got on the Net looking for temples (specifically Shirdi Sai Temple in New South Wales). Joyce found it. There were other staff members and me in the room. Suddenly, the computer started playing Om loudly. We were all startled but laughed. I was in absolute joy at having found a Shirdi Temple, in Sydney, Australia.

Second Leela: I put myself out to go to Westfield at lunch to get away from the desk. On the way I looked up at a clear, beautiful blue sky and there was Swami's jet stream. I felt better knowing that the Babas knew of yet another despairing day at work. One day I will find (with Baba's grace) a job where I will be truly happy.

20 May

Not being able to contain my joy, and wanting to go to the Temple immediately, I managed to get the number and address of the Shirdi Temple in North Strathfield. At noon aarti, the temple pictures in the puja room lit up. At first I looked, blinked the eyes and looked again only to receive the sweetest darshan from the pictures and from my Shirdi on the wall. I felt such a sadness that I knew that Shirdi Baba was there, but I still had a strong desire, to see Him in the flesh. After aarti, the eyes of Baba in the portrait looked piercingly into my eyes. I consoled myself to await more conversations with and from Him. Saburi Lorraine!

Leela (30 May)

PN and Shirdi are ever on my mind. If it were my will, I would go today. At aarti I asked Baba to send me something personal directly from Him or allow me to experience a small leela, as well as (greedy me) a sign telling me if I may go to Shirdi and PN. At Liverpool station, I saw a bus with the word 'Travel' on it. This has always been in the past. Baba sends His sign/approval (the word 'Travel') in this way so that I may make arrangements for the trip. I was very happy, but I realised that I will have to save, (what with the GST [a form of tax]), and all depended on Baba's grace. I also went to the New Age Shop at Westfield and picked up a free paper from the floor. On reading it on the way home, the words stood out 'Sathya Sai Speaks' by Jack Roper. I was ecstatic. Another sign to go. I went to the post-office this morning to get stamps. While in queue, I looked up to see a very striking photo of Jesus looking down at me. I gave Him a smile and a quiet 'hello'. He looked exquisite.

June

Dream (17 June)

At last I saw Baba in my dream. I thought I was given the flick, such despair! Short dream, but my Baba was very clearly there. As usual, I was in a crowd doing many things with many people. I saw a picture with Baba sitting sideways in a chair. I was elated to see Baba in our midst. On looking at the picture again, Baba came alive, turned around and blessed me and all with both hands. Oh joy!

July

Shirdi Sansthan (8 July)

I had Shirdi Baba on my mind, (what was new). I had a short dream (my excitement at going to a bhajan Sansthan at a friend's place tonight). In my dream I saw Shirdi Baba sitting in His usual leg pose in the form of a statue, on an altar. I went up close to the statue and suddenly He was alive. Then I awoke. I prayed that Baba never left me.

Darshan (15 July)

I got a bump on the head from the printer, and had a headache. At noon aarti, my head was still throbbing. I lay the eyes on Shirdi Baba's big picture in the puja room. What a beautiful sight to behold! The eyes rolled and changed colour. Even the 'Om' on Baba's hand had a white Light shining from it. I was grateful and so glad.

Dreams Relating to God Are Real—Sathya Sai Baba (29 July)

I was determined to slowly go off all the three medications (for high blood pressure and high cholesterol) and go natural, and with this idea in mind, I did not take medication last night. It took me a while to sleep but when I did, I finally drifted off and was happy to have had an answer dream from my beloved Baba of Shirdi. Prior to sleep and also during the day, I asked Baba to appear before me, yet again, if He was with me. No, I didn't lack faith, just patience and intelligence and a frustration that I felt so very close to Shirdi Baba but cannot see Him as a human. At least with Sathya Sai, on going to India, I do get good darshan and more of our beloved Swami. With Shirdi Baba, though I know He is with me, I longed for

Him and cannot see Him bodily every day, except when His pictures come alive on occasions.

I had a dream. I was in a very strangely built house, with different levels, and was complaining to Mum because there was dirty water pouring forth in the bathroom and we could not settle as it was in a mess. Suddenly, three or four women came to me selling pictures. I bought, without looking at any of them, a bundle of the pictures and paid the women with some very shiny coins. Glimpsing through the pictures, I was very happy to see one of my beloved Baba of Shirdi in His white kafni and another picture of Him, His head only with a cap on, peeking at me from a wall. I kept telling everyone that even though it was only Baba's head peeping from behind the wall, He was watching us.

I know You are ever watchful my Beloved Baba, if only I could experience Thee in flesh now, but I will have to have saburi and thank You for the dream.

August

Vibhuti Dream (3 August)

I had a dream that I was in a shop which was selling mounds of ready-made vibhuti. I went to a lady shopping there and told her to go to Swami for vibhuti as He materialised the same and not to buy it from the shop. Then I looked at my own hand to see vibhuti spurting out of my fingers. I gathered it in my right hand and placed it in my pocket. I awoke. It was a pity that there was no vibhuti on my hands when I awoke.

Another Dream (4 August)

Amidst a crowd of people sitting together talking, in my dream I noticed a lady wearing a shawl sitting near me. On her small finger was a ring with an image. It looked exactly like the ring with my Shirdi Baba on it that I wear on my small finger. I, as usual, got very happy and asked her about the ring. She said it was not Shirdi but her own guru, whose name sounded very much like Paramhansa Yogananda. I noticed again that she was wearing another ring and that had a picture on it that resembled `PN. I remained quiet. The dream continued with me receiving two bars of chocolate. I think it is time to go to Shirdi and Parthy again. I am now waiting for the 'Yes' signs from You.

6 August

At noon aarti I had a very pleasant surprise indeed. I received darshan from Shirdi Baba's middle picture on the altar. The left eye moved first, my heart skipped several beats, as this was the only picture that gave the darshan. May the peace of the Lord reign on all. Then the most beautiful darshan was given by the Babas while I was doing japa in the lounge. Shirdi Sai glowed. The face was masked by Divine Light so I could only see the Light and not Baba's face. Swami came to Light, I felt as though Swami was about to speak. He looked alive, very young and smiled ever so gently and peacefully. The Babas radiated Light, peace and pure Divine love.

Divine Leela (12 August)

'Music doth soothe the savage beast', so the saying goes. In my attempt to soothe my feverish brain, I tried to play the very beautiful 'Sai Gopala' CD—it worked.

Thank You my Babas at least one very important piece of equipment worked, most of the electrical gear at home does not work. I love this CD and whoever sings the bhajans, do so rather mellifluously. Thank You again, the Babas.

Vibhuti (18 August)

I always feel and weep alone when I am ill or have to take tests. I broke down at work. I went to the back to finish a report. I was alone, I got the strongest smell of vibhuti. When Claire came back, I asked her if she was using a perfume to which she replied 'No'. The smell wafted in and out. I knew it was the Babas but was hesitant to admit the same as I have not smelt vibhuti for a very long time. When I got home, at the front door, the smell was there again and very strong. I realised my Babas were telling me, 'Have no fear, Baba is here'.

24 August

I was very nervous about the dentist whom I were to visit the following day. I asked Baba to be with me and to be the dentist because I knew He could, and He would not cause me any pain. I was delighted to receive on Thursday vibhuti and sugar from *Shirdi in India* in the mail. This was an assurance from Baba that He was with me. After receiving the vibhuti, a very strong smell of it followed me from the letter box into the house.

25 August

I awoke early, calm but fearful. The driver, Patrick, a Scotsman picked me up in the silver tarrago car. I nearly fell over when I saw him. He was in his 60s, white-haired and very similar looking to my Shirdi Sai, but without the scarf, (I chuckled to myself, at last Baba has appeared in human form, but He forgot to wear His scarf). It is a pity I could not take a photo of Patrick as the likeness to Baba was uncanny. He observed my nervous state in the car on the way to the dentist and was very reassuring. He dropped me at the desk, assuring me again that he would pick me up and drop me home safely after the treatment. I had my vibhuti in my pocket and kept chanting '*Sai Sai*'. After my dental procedure under anaesthetic, the driver Patrick drove me home and made sure I was safe. I don't remember a thing, no pain, no vomit just peaceful sleep. Patrick delivered me into the house, kept the keys safely by the door, and left, which he confirmed the next time I saw him. I have to mention here that I was anaesthetised at the dentist and they have a service whereby if you have no one to pick you up or drop you off home after your procedure, their driver Patrick does this job. He was a very safe, efficient and trustworthy person who also cared a lot for sick patients. This was a courtesy service provided by the dentist.

Alika was supposed to come over that night with soup and champagne. As usual on the phone, she always told me to *live life*. I do believe this is a very direct message from Baba to me.

The Divine Light—The Olympic Torch (28 August)

I awoke early this morning. Daylight saving has started early due to the Olympics (from October to March we have Daylight Saving, where the clock is placed an hour forward and at the approach of winter, it is rewound an hour back, to normal hours. During the Olympics, DA started in September. After saying 'Oms' twenty-one times at 4.00 a.m., I turned off the light and just lay in bed. Then I noticed the little 'dancing angels' all over the bedroom, flying merrily around, even coming close to the eyes. I asked Baba if what I was seeing was the effulgent Divine Light. I told him that I was going to switch the TV on, and if I immediately saw any form of light, it would be His answer to me. I turned on the TV, the Olympic Flame was going past. *Sai Ram.*

Dream (31 August)

It looked like an auditorium. I was about to be seated. I saw Swami approaching with some people at His side. He stood in front of me and said, 'Take this Lorraine, for you' and something else, which I don't remember. I was so surprised and happy I don't recall the other words. Swami gave me *(a)* a packet of vibhuti, *(b)* a packet with the words manuka honey (amrit) on it, and *(c)* a photograph of myself with a dark thing or person beside me. I was so happy I just kept saying, 'He knew my name, He called me by my name.' Swami walked around for a while, then I awoke. The dream ended here.

September

What a Happy Day Today! (11 September)

It was very kind of my darling mother Connie who came to the airport to see me off. Thank you dear mother of mine and God Bless you. I went through a fierce storm on the way to Bangalore, (as mentioned before, I do not like flying or storms and to have both at the same time, was more than fearsome, but I always carry my *Sai Satcharita* and a little brass statue of Shirdi Sai along with pictures and crosses of Jesus, courtesy my dear mother, she makes sure that I carry her end of the heavenly beings as well as pictures of Swami) but was not scared as He was with me. I prayed quietly and we landed safely. I was very tired, and stayed at Bangalore at the lovely St. Marks. I visited the Ulsoor Temple, Mysore and Srirangapatnam. As usual, Hagalappa, was in the supine position while the orphans worked. He was the custodian of the Sathya Sai Orphanage at Srirangapatnam, near Mysore. They also had a temple at the orphanage where after a miniscule puja was performed for the visitor, money donations were asked for by Hagalappa. Then he used to go back to his bed to stay there for the rest of the day until the next visitor came. It was an effort for him to get off his bed, but I made sure he did. I was given a bottle of amrit and vibhuti. I thought that the bees must have been working overtime to produce the amrit. My beloved Shirdi Sai was still in the wooden box waiting to be taken out. This annoyed me further, and Hagalappa was told off again by me. Shirdi Sai was not a bird to be caged. The statue of Baba had been there for months in a crate. It was about time that the temple be completed. Five or six years had passed and the progress was very slow, I wondered what happened to all the funds he collected; he certainly did not have to pay servants to do his work, it is the poor children/orphans who did it anyway, and they were so sweet, always smiling and obliging.

Mysore (13 September)
I visited the deaf children at The Sisters of Mercy, a very beautiful convent and even more beautiful were the children who were taken care of by such compassionate nuns. I loved them all. We had such a happy, though brief time together as I had to get back to Bangalore that night. With God's grace I hoped to meet them again.

It was a horror drive back to Bangalore. It was 8 p.m. I was frazzled. The next day I had gone to see Baba at Ulsoor. I was running late but was blessed to witness most of the Abshishekam. He looked resplendent, surrounded by hundreds of devotees, wearing His gold crown. I felt like I was in the Chavadi in Shirdi.

Parthy (14 September)
On the way to Parthy, I stopped at the beautiful Shirdi Sai Temple near Chikkabellapatnam (hope I have the name right here), took lots of photographs of Baba and was given some prasad. Then on to Puttaparthi where there was no room at the Ashram due to a conference, so I stayed at Sai Sadan. I liked it here, Shirdi Sai and Sathya Sai were up in the puja room (a private puja room on the sixth floor of the hotel, where bhajans are sometimes held and where one can worship or sit in silent meditation while staying at the hotel) above my room and so was a beautiful murti of Lord Ganesha. I loved Ganesha, He was like a big friend of mine and I also chatted with statues and pictures of Him occasionally. I have been luckily given a lot of Ganesha statues by friends.

Darshan (15 September)
I was a bit nervous to venture out alone at 5 a.m. but by Baba's grace I met Nita at the front door of the hotel on her way to the Nilayam. We shared a trishaw and she paid Rs10 (she said it was the host country and I was a guest). How kind was she and still better as she was from Pune (close to Shirdi country). I had a beautiful darshan from the tenth row. Swami looked very serene and my tears welled once again in gratitude for Him being here. After breakfast, I bought three roses for my beloved Shirdi in the garden.

It was very humid I tried to have a nap in the afternoon. The whole room was filled with a magnificent fragrance which lasted for at least an hour.

Leelas (16 September)

I did not go early today as I was exhausted with the heat. I went at 7.30 a.m. to find all the gates closed. I was told that Swami was on His way to meet a VIP. I stood on the street with the rest of the crowd, noticing a white Mercedes approaching with Anil Kumar, Swami's personal interpreter, in the front, getting a mere glimpse of Swami's hair at the back. That was enough to put a smile on my face. At breakfast, a lady sitting across the table from me was reading a book on my beloved Shirdi Sai. I received darshan from His photo on the cover of the book. He was ever with me.

Getting Closer and Closer (19 September)

I was sitting against the wall. This was a good place to be as one could see Swami coming in from His house, when the music started. Before Swami came in, I uttered a small request, 'Please give us a wave Swami'. On His way in, He stopped for a second, raised His divine hand and waved. Well, what can I say except thank Swami. *Sai Ram.*

Line 1 (24 September)

I was in line 3. I nagged and complained to Swami but was mesmerised when Swami glided in and stood right in front of us for a few seconds. He looked so sweet and loving. I bought two books at the store and was handed a marigold by the cashier. He placed it on the books with a smile on his face. I placed it in my hair with a smile. It was a gift from the Babas as I had earlier asked for a blessing (marigolds, jai and jui—the flowers mentioned in the *Sai Satcharita*—that Baba used to water and planted by Baba in His garden). After bhajans on the way to the gate, I noticed a lot of ladies standing near the mandir. I also stood with them, they were entering the temple. I did too, my first time ever, very happy to be doing so and even happier when I saw a beautiful murti of my beloved Shirdi Sai. His eyes glistened and He looked so divine. I was very touched, and thankful to Him for having granted me a much longed for entrance into the temple and was doubly graced by seeing my Shirdi Sai in there.

25 September

Thank You Swami for Parthy, till, as I prayed, we meet again soon.

Shirdi (26 September)

The drive to Shirdi was horrendous with so many near misses, the traffic and the chaos. I got to 'Sun-n-Sand' at 11 a.m. It was very hot and smelly. I had no sleep for thirty-six hours and I was very hungry, but my Beloved was there. I had ordered a chocolate cake for Shirdi Sai, as His birthday was on 28 September. The hotel management went into shock. They had never heard of such a request for a cake, but after much ado, the cook decided to try his best to accommodate my quaint request. Before retiring for the night, I looked at His beautiful portrait in the room. I was graced by His darshan from the portrait. My hair stood on end and this had happened so for a few more times that day. This was my heaven on earth, I loved Him so as does everyone there. I thought He was also very excited about the cake that was why He had given me so much darshan from the painting in my room.

Shirdi Leelas (27 September)

I awoke after a fantastic sleep to such a glorious day.

Leela 1: I could not eat the toast at breakfast, it was too hard. I was complaining to Baba about the same, when the doorbell rang. There was a waiter at the door with a plate of fresh, soft croissants. His Kindness! He even looked after my teeth and swallowing, which were a mess after having radiotherapy. It is very difficult to chew anything hard, as the teeth easily break, and having no saliva, swallowing is also difficult.

Leela 2: The manager rang to say the cook had agreed to bake the cake. I thought all the hotel staff were excited about the cake and the birthday as much as I was. I visited the Sansthan. After paying my respects at the Samadhi, where He looked as beautiful as always, I visited the Sansthan offices seeking their help in finding me a guide to take me around Shirdi. Having no luck, (they don't supply guides and neither can you hire one), I left in frustration. I closed my eyes and said, 'Baba, it would be lovely to have a guide to take me through the village'. I opened my eyes to see a sadhu (holy man) standing near me, asking in a language of sorts if I required a guide; I did recognise the word guide. Here was my Shirdi Sai in the form of this guide, answering my prayer. The guide (wearing orange) led me to all the right places and even though he did not speak English, I understood him perfectly. A lot of the places I visited are named in the *Sai Satcharita* and many of the devotees mentioned in the book, have their descendents still living in Shirdi. I met Mahalsapathy's (the foremost disciple of Baba) two great grandchildren, managed to see Baba's kafni and satka which was given to Mahalsapathy and which was enclosed in a glass case. The guide took me to another Baba devotee (when Baba was in His mortal coil) Baijabai's house. She used to feed Baba. I saw Baba's horse Shyamarkna's tomb, as well as the Padukas under the sacred neem tree and Lendi Bagh which was so very beautiful, and had been redone having a water feature in it. I visited Abdul Baba's tomb (another very close devotee of Baba) and his house too and was blessed in the Muslim way by a relative of Abdul Baba. I felt very close to Abdul, who was very much like my Shirdi Sai and was loved by Baba. Thank You my beloved guide, my beloved Baba. Such a Divine day!

Happy Birthday to My Beloved Everything (28 September)

The cake was brought into my room in a box, how sweet were the people here. We took it to the Samadhi (main temple wherein lies the tomb) and presented it to the pujari (priest) who looked shocked. One normally presents coconuts, roses and the like to Baba, never a cake. After blessing the cake, I made sure I took a knife from the hotel kitchen, sliced the cake at the altar (with the whole hundreds of devotees looking on in awe) and gave it to the pujari for my Baba. The pujari (they are normally very stern) also took a piece and laughed aloud. My heart fluttered. My Baba had accepted the chocolate birthday cake. Then the pujari gave me a bunch of roses from very near to Baba's statue. Happy birthday my beloved Baba. I shared the cake with all who could grab some.

I went to Dwarakamai and rested the back against the pole that my Baba used to lean against. I realised that my back already felt much better and the pain disappeared. Then I visited the Khandoba Temple. I felt so loved that day. I went for aarti at 9.00 p.m. The place was filled with hundreds of people. I felt Baba's presence. I watched the Chavadi procession. The Chavadi procession as in the *Sai Satcharita*, is still observed on Thursdays in Shirdi, where a beautiful life-like portrait of Baba is carried from Dwarakamai to the Chavadi where Baba is laid to rest for the night. For me, it felt like I was actually watching this very scene with Baba Himself in the Palki, in the days when His body was on earth. It is unexplainable the closeness that I feel sometimes to Baba. The Palki bearers were in their uniforms and it was such a serene sight to behold. Our beloved Maharaj was carried from the mandir to the Chavadi to rest for the night. I even managed to get (with His grace of course) a seat in the Chavadi while the rituals were performed.

Leaving Shirdi (29 September)
I was not sad to leave Shirdi, knowing that my Baba was ever with me. I dearly love this place and pray that He brought me back soon. It was a very hot and scary trip. I stopped to get some fruits. I was carrying the amrit received at Srirangapatanam with me. A thought suddenly came to me and I asked, 'Swami, is the amrit real or fake, please let me know'. I got into the car and was about to drive off, when another car pulled in with the words 'Real'. Thank You Swami. I ended this journey of much love with my sincere thanks to Shirdi Sai, Sathya Sai, Jesus Sai and Our Holy Mother too, for everything.

October

Back Home in Australia—A Strange Event (17 October)
I fell asleep around 9.30 p.m. but at about 10.15 p.m., I thought I heard the phone ring. I awoke suddenly and the ringing stopped. I got back under the doona and looked at the ceiling for some unknown reason. I was fully awake by that time, seeing a string of snakes falling upon me. I actually screamed aloud and hid under the covers. I fell back to sleep and got up later to check for the snakes. There were none. *Om Namah Shiva.*

Dream (20 October)
Just before waking, I was in a crowd of people, and there was a very large pandal. I could see two pictures—one of my beloved Shirdi Sai and a smaller one of our beloved Sathya Sai. While I was very happy to see the pictures, I was complaining that they should have been bigger, like the pandal. Then another dream followed but I vaguely remember the same. There was a picture with blue skies, a sick girl sitting near me. We were looking at a picture of Swami, when another lady who came in on a man's shoulder, went up to the picture and painted some white clouds on the blue sky

and everyone clapped. The girl turned to me and whispered, 'Pray for me, I am dying'. I could see Swami from afar and could hear bells ringing. I awoke very gently and while awakening could still hear the beautiful sound of the bells ringing.

Beautiful Leela/Deepavali (27 October)

For some reason this morning, when I was praying to Lord Ganapati, I requested that I be showered with roses today by Shirdi Baba, and Ganesh should help out too. I also reminded Shirdi of the same, just a gesture that He was with me. I sometimes 'out of the blue' make strange requests to Baba. Before I left the house, I stated 'I won't be greedy, one rose will be sufficient to show me that You love me'. On entering the consult room, getting it ready for the Clinic, I was very surprised to see a beautiful basket of silk roses on the desk, I took one as I felt this was from my beloved Shirdi Sai to me. I was told later it was made by an Italian woman patient with chronic Multiple Sclerosis to thank us. I have one rose taken home by me, from such a big beautiful basket of silk roses. I did believe that it was placed there by Shirdi Sai answering my request to Him. I love You and I thank You my sweet Sai.

November

Spider Bite (3 November)

I felt a sharp pain on the right leg. Looking at the spot, I could see the flesh pierced, a bit of blood oozing. Something had bitten me. I took no notice of it. Before reaching the Mall to shop, I was in a lather of sweat. It came on suddenly and left just as suddenly. Then at night the sweat came on again, then again on Saturday morning. There was no other symptoms, except the sweat and a fever which I also had on Thursday. On thinking of this, I realised and felt in my heart that I had been bitten by a spider, but I have been saved by a worse fate by the Babas. I put vibhuti on the wound and asked the Babas to take it away. Also, if this was really a spider bite, as the sweats and fevers were indications of the same, and since the Babas had saved me, I requested Them to give me a sign of this beautiful leela. It came in the form of the most beautiful darshan. This really happened to me, and I still have a scar on my leg. We have some deadly species of spiders in Australia, even in homes in summer.

First Bhajan   20 September 97

Author on first visit to Shirdi with guide who appeared/disappeared after the Shirdi tour

Shiva Tree Flowers   10 October 2001

Author distributing rice

Painting of Baba on rock in gardern at Prashanthi Nilayam, Puttaparthi

'The Pink Picture' in altar room

Thayeeamma's Temple
This is the Murti from which Baba's hand in spirit
form had put a flower in the author's hand

Healing (4 November)

At noon prayers, I felt very blessed to have attained the most beautiful darshan of practically the whole altar. I was ever so happy to have received the most amazing darshan from the bronze statue of Shirdi Sai, Shirdi on the wall. I felt like He was about to *jump off the wall*. Swami's face glowed, the lingam moved, Shirdi Sai's sacred feet glowed. I was humbled and felt grateful. This was my sign from Baba that I was healed of the spider bite. My *koti koti pranaams* to You, my most beloved Babas. Thank You also—Jesus, Our Lady, and everyone in the puja room. As mentioned earlier, spiders in Australia like the red back and a few others, can have fatal effects if a person is bitten. I don't know exactly what spider I was bitten by, but I do know what I saw, the leg swelling, the immediate fever and the sweats.

2001

A very happy new year to all. *Sai Ram*.

January

1 January

I couldn't wait to get to bed tonight after all the 'partying'. I was relaxing with the *Women's Weekly* when I got the strongest smell of vibhuti. I sniffed hard and long to make sure. Yes, it was vibhuti. Happy Merry Millennium to the Babas! From the first day of the year, it was clear to me that it would be another year filled with Your joyous blessings and love for me.

There was no ego here, just hope.

12 January

Rang Rajshree was a dear friend of mine. After wishing her on the phone on her birthday, Raj was more excited about the dream she had had about Shirdi Sai just before waking, and that too on her birthday. She interpreted the dream thus: she saw Baba sitting on His rock. He walked towards her and even though His mouth never moved, she heard the words 'Everything you hear about Me is true'. This was the end of Rajs' dream. What beautiful grace from Baba on one's birthday!

Dream (21 January)

I saw in my dream that there was a gathering in a field. The ladies were dressed in beautiful colourful sarees. A friend handed me an empty plate and said something to me, I didn't know what. I noticed Radha looking very refreshed but thin and was angry that his back was sore. I was right at the back, but could see Swami from that distance standing before a table/microphone wearing His orange robe. I was frustrated being so far back and vented my anger that I wasn't closer to Swami even though I could see His orange robe and hair. My dream ended.

30 January

Before leaving for work today, I asked Swami to give me darshan of Himself or any sign to show me that I was still in His good books. I stepped out on the street. It was 7 a.m. The very first thing I saw walking towards me was a lovely Indian (we don't have any Indians living in our street) lady in a long white dress strolling by. I smiled at her, she looked at me with Swami's eyes and said, 'Good Morning'. Thank You Swami, it was You. And there was more. On the train, while going to work as well as on returning home, I saw the word 'Sai' scribbled. I realised that I was still in His good books. I prayed that the Babas indulged me and filled this diary every day or perhaps once a week with Their grace, darshan, *sparshan* and *sambhasan. Sai Ram.*

February

Grace (10 February)

At aarti this morning, I mentioned casually to Baba, 'it would be nice to meet someone—anyone, from Shirdi today'. My sister Cherryl rang me to say Hazel was here (a friend who lives in London). Hazel used to live in Nagpur, (close to Shirdi). Yes, He did send someone who lived close to Shirdi. Then the most precious moment of all was when I was doing japa in the lounge, I received the darshan of the Babas. I was grateful and thankful.

Grace (18 February)

At bhajans, with my croaky voice and amid tears, I asked Swami for a flower. It would be nice to see one fall. Nothing happened during bhajans, but on the way out, I found a beautiful gardenia (my most favourite flower) fresh and lovely on the grass. Thank You my beloved Swami. At noon aarti in the puja room, the most beautiful face of Shirdi Sai gave out the most beautiful darshan. Baba's hand with the 'Aum' sign glowed, so did His face, lasting for about three minutes. I was in awe. I can only once again humbly say Thank You Baba. I do love You so and please don't stop loving me.

20 February

I have been reading *Messages from My Dearest Friend Sai Baba* by Elvie Bailey. I prayed that I too would be so blessed (Lisa too) with the grace, love, bliss, blessings of the Lord soon. Sharon, my younger sister, rang and we conversed for an hour. At one stage during our conversation the lounge room was filled with the smell of the fragrant vibhuti. It was appreciated.

21 February

It was Mahashivaratri. I prayed that Lisa and I be blessed with a miracle from Lord Shiva today and I actually experienced a small leela. I always found it difficult to wear the Indian earrings, and ended up putting them away in sheer frustration. Quietly, I prayed to my Sweet Lord to help me get them on. There was no struggle, and I could put them on easily. I thanked Baba requesting Him for a supreme leela, being the special day that it was.

22 February

I fell off to sleep about 2 a.m., but was happy to be able to do the Shiva nama japa. I was tossing, turning the lights off and on, and questioning to the Babas, 'Why are You not helping me to go to sleep? You know I have to start a new job tomorrow'. I don't know why I was kept awake, but I was. At one stage (about 1.30 a.m.) I turned off the lamp yet again, only to see the 'large white clouds' coming from the puja room. They were very thick and pretty and even turned blue, so in my exhaustion, I cried, 'Ah the angels are here'. They did not stay too long, my eyes being extremely tired to focus. Just before falling into slumber I asked 'Baba, did You just send the angels, if so, clear my sight and knock three times, but before I fall off to sleep'. Knock, knock, knock, though faint, I heard it. Thank You my Baba, now I know why I had to stay awake. Mahashivaratri—may the Grace of God fall on Lisa and me forevermore.

At work I was outside eating lunch, when I met this young couple from Sri Lanka. We started to talk, I was so happy, on exchanging pleasantries to see the bride wearing Swami's ring and chain. Baba allowed me to bless them with vibhuti and pictures. *Sai Ram.*

March

The Fire (1 March)

I was very tired. I was in a very deep sleep when about 11.00p.m., even while sleeping, I heard a 'Tic Tic' sound quite loud, which awoke me. I saw the candle near Baba's painting alight the flame being very high, and the cloth on the table having caught fire. I jumped out of bed trying to blow it out, nearly burning my face. With Baba's grace and timely warning, the cloth stopped burning and the candle went out. This was odd as I light a candle here every day before going to bed. This had never happened before. After the event, Baba very kindly graced me with sweet slumber. It had not stopped me from lighting candles here; still do it, as He is ever watching and protecting me.

4 March

At bhajans today at our Centre, for the first time, I went into deep meditation. At one stage I could feel the white light pouring into me, even though the eyes were closed. It was very peaceful. On opening the eyes I noticed Swami's Lotus Feet were white, with two very red toes. I had to look a few times to see if they were still white. After a few minutes, the Lotus Feet turned back to its normal colour.

Darshan—Smell of Vibhuti (30 March)

I was feeling like the body does not belong to me. Legs racked with pain as was the left side of the head. I finished reading *Nandana* which was written by Swami's students. During the reading I had some beautiful fragrance of vibhuti. At 5.15 p.m. I was doing japa, praying to the Babas to show me that they were with me. My prayer was answered almost immediately. I got the most beautiful darshan from Swami's portrait near the entrance to the house.

April

Ram Navami (2 April)

I have read in the *Sai Satcharita* about the Ram Navami festival, not realising that I would be a part of it one day. Kala and I went to the same at the Minto temple. We were welcomed by our dear friends Sue and Dan. Dan made the huge pot of pilaf, for a crowd of about 200 people. I was thrilled to see the 'cradle' with Lord Rama in it, the Ramayana was kept opened on the altar. I did aarti to Hanuman, Ganesh, Rama, and was feeling very happy. My Shirdi had never left my thoughts as He had brought the Ram Navami and Urus together. These occasions made me feel even closer to Him. I was being guided spiritually by Baba to witness whatever was written in the *Satcharita*. I was also literally filled with beautiful prasad as food, good company and immense happiness.

Leelas—Full Room (8 April)

In my usual rough manner after prayers, yesterday, I urged Swami to come back. 'My Shirdi Baba is everything, but You Swami, Jesus and God's team are a breath behind'. After bhajans this morning, I visited Kala and Henry to pick up some things. Kala gave me another book, *Love Is My Form*, the first of the ten volumes written by R. Padmanaban. The most beautifully illustrated black/white biography of the first years of Swami's life (1926–50). It is truly beautiful. Swami re-entered in a *big way*, and I requested Him never to leave as asked earlier. Most of the day was spent enthralled in this captivating book.

9 April

The angels flew around and were in abundance today. I keep wondering to myself 'Am I crazy, is it my eyes or are these really Divine beings'. Some of them came right above, up close and almost touching the eyes. I could not sleep. I was very tired, perhaps the eyes were playing tricks on me. I could also hear little utterances and mutterings. I got a bit scared, so I kept the light on for most of the night. The angels disappeared, stared at the ceiling and said, 'God if these are really angels that I see, I am glad of their visit, but give me a sign that they are by leaving a feather somewhere'.

Feather Story Continued (10 April)

Before leaving for Katoomba, I searched for a feather in the bedroom and everywhere else, but there was nothing. God has His own time.

I had a very 'happy day' with Mum and Cheryl in Leura. I found Mum's Menorrha, so I bought it for her. She certainly deserved it and wanted it so much! Still no feathers were found, this did not keep me from looking for the sign.

The Feather (12 April)

I had a dreadful night, no sleep. I read the papers till 3.30 a.m., finally dozed off for about half an hour. I was about to make the bed after aarti, when I found the cutest little feather just between the bed and the cupboard. I burst into laughter. God did answer me. They were angels, the clouds that flew around the bedroom sometimes. I thanked God and hoped His Divine beings (my divine friends) would be with me forevermore. What a very sweet leela! I asked for a feather and got my proof.

29 April

A moment of bliss. At the Study Circle, which was indeed very interesting, as the discussion was about humans forming/merging with God, our moments of bliss which, according to most, were our emotions, not bliss bombs provided by God. This led me to wonder about the moments; the minutes and times I had experienced with the Babas were they just my emotions. Take for instance, the noon aarti just performed, where I prayed 'I love You God, show me Your love for me', I had the most beautiful darshan from my beloved Shirdi's picture in the puja room. He was rolling His eyes and looking at me, then the lovely white light took over His beautiful face. I was mesmerised. My euphoria only abated after the white light disappeared, I realised Baba was back in spirit. True Bliss! was this an emotion? The eyes saw very clearly, that what was before me, what took place before me, emotions like tears and joy did follow, this is my clarification of emotions, i.e., tears and joy, but to witness something so clearly, for me this was no emotion.

Abundance (30 April)

Did the Angel Cards about 2–3 days ago and picked the card of *abundance?* Left it in front of Baba's portrait and thought, I would change the card today. I shuffled, affirmed then with eyes closed, mind on the angels chose a card from the middle—*abundance* again. This for me was God and good sign. I hoped to have abundance in every area of my life, particularly God's grace. Happy Birthday Lord Buddha. May You too abundantly be with me.

May

5 May

Kala and I (accompanied by you know who, Shirdi Sai of course, if you still don't know) went to the Festival of Mind, Body and Spirit in Darling Harbour. I bought Masala Tea bags from Africa, vegan chips, a red pashmina, red lipstick, heard some beautiful music, ate delicious lunch (fat chips! Guacomole, etc.) orange juice (organic), strawberry/cream, and we really had such fun and lovely time, and satwic food! There was a huge thunderstorm and it poured all day.

At one of the stalls I was delighted to see my Shirdi Sai standing out in a picture. I squealed in delight. (I either scream or laugh aloud with profound joy, no matter what part or place of the world I am in, if I see a picture or statue of Shirdi Baba. I call it 'spontaneous delight'). I asked the lady if it was for sale. She said 'No' and she asked me if I knew who He was in the picture. I said 'Yes, I wear Him on my finger and carry Him in my heart'. Around 4.30 we had to leave even though it was still pouring and we had no umbrellas. It was lovely to walk in the rain though and thank You God for such a gloriously happy day and Your beautiful darshan, my Baba. I told you He came too and was ever with me.

Beautiful Darshan (6 May)

Happy Birthday Eswaramma and Dad. I had a lazy day. It was raining so stayed home and 'pigged out' on chocolate and ice cream (satwic food!), besides it was the last day of my-six week vacation. I will have to be back to work tomorrow in another new job. I was doing japa in the lounge, Swami 'Lit up'. Shirdi Sai was hesitant at first, but did make a brief appearance. My hair stood on end many times, Swami's face was so alive and so alight, I was hoping They would step out of the picture. I felt very happy.

Dream (28 May)

I was reading *Love is My Form* where Swami says '*He is always with us*'. Before sleeping I asked Him to show me if He was with me. I had a dream. I saw Swami come out and put some things on the floor, where a small group of people had gathered. Swami distributed things to them, I wanted it too, but Swami looked at me sternly and said, 'write a letter, later, later'. Swami then threw huge bags of vibhuti everywhere, so I grabbed one of them, I was very sad at being ignored by Swami, so close and yet so far. Next I saw Swami going towards a long chair and sitting on it. I saw Cheryl my sister, going and sitting beside Him. Next I saw Swami talking to Trevor (my ex-husband), who looked puzzled as he could not understand what Swami was saying. As usual I was upset, being ignored by Swami. My dream ended here.

June

Gifts (16 June)

I asked Baba to give me a gift from Him to me this morning, any gift. I was cleaning the puja room, about time too, as usual staring and chatting with Shirdi Sai and looking into His eyes. It looked like a tiger and was staring back at me. His eyes were luminescent. I was baking for the next day. I looked out at the clouds. There were two distinct-shaped hearts. I moved the bowl for washing, on picking it up I was happy to see that the flour that fell from the sifter was a distinct 'Om'. Thank You God for Your treasured and sweet gifts. It never ended there though. I got beautiful darshan in the lounge and the angels came at night, one particularly with a mighty force. I think this was Michael the Archangel. Such Grace in abundance!

18 June

I spent the day searching for the word 'Michael', but had no luck. I almost gave up searching for the word 'Michael'. I went to pick up my dry cleaning. On the way back, I saw a noticeboard with a flyer on it in bright orange, which of course got my attention immediately. The first word on it was Michael.

Last night, the angels appeared briefly. I was irate, as I could not sleep and was very restless. I kept mumbling to the angels. Just before passing out with exhaustion I could feel cool air blowing on my face. I told the angels, 'wrong air, it should be hot, now being winter'. Then I fell into deep slumber. Was that Shirdi Sai? My heart told me it was Him coming in that form. If it be Thee, then show me.

God's Gift (21 June)

Every morning on waking, I talk to my Shirdi Sai asking Him to give me a gift (i.e., grace) no matter what it may be. I would recognise it as being heaven-sent. Before setting off for work, I was standing at the kitchen window having a cup of coffee, admiring nature, i.e., the sky. One area of the sky was bright blue, another area bright pink, the pink glow being so strong that the kitchen became pink. I did not heed it too much, being in a hurry to leave, and god, Oh God, not one but two bright and beautiful rainbows! I felt like God was saying, 'Here Lorraine, I am here'. I could only humbly say, 'Thank You for the beauty that You created in nature'.

And Another Gift (22 June)

On the way to work, I was always happy to see the beautiful birds, sitting, chit-chatting, flying and gracing the earth with their beautiful colours. I have seen a lot of green parrots who were very pretty, but the two I saw that morning, I felt I was looking at Shirdi Sai and Sathya Sai themselves, wearing coats of indescribable vibrant hues. Parrots were not long birds; these two were on a low branch, very long in body and oh the colours! They too seemed to look at me and call me.

23 June

During the bhajans, at my home today, the altar looked beautiful, the singers crooned their best, the food was in abundance, thanks to all who cooked so much, most of all thank You God, for a very happy evening indeed. After bhajans we had a lovely satsang. The candle burned on till Monday morning. I was exhausted after the bhajans last night here, as when it was over I did not go to sleep, staying up all night in front of the altar, praying. Therefore I was feeling extremely tired today but extremely happy.

The Picture (30 June)

Concern for the deaf children in Mysore had always been at the back of my mind. How do I get some money to them. I left my worry at Baba's Feet. I had lunch with Mum in the City, then noticed a very small shop with the bold yellow/black lettering Western Union. I went towards the window where behind it stood an Indian guy. I enquired about sending money through them to the children in Mysore, when my eyes caught my beloved Shirdi Sai's picture sitting on their filing cabinet. I screamed with delight and blew kisses to Him, (not the man at the counter, but my Shirdi Sai). My mother stood stunned, so did the poor man behind the counter. What more can I say except how very much I loved You. You make me so happy in Your sweet simple way and I thank You and love You. The money was sent to the School for Deaf Children, and I got my Shirdi Sai's darshan quite unexpectedly. Every time I go past Western Union at Town Hall Station in the City, I try never to forget about Baba's darshan first, making sure I walk past Western Union, just to get a glimpse from Him and in return give Him a smile and a wave. Whenever the fellow behind the counter notices me walking by, he chuckles.

July

Grace/Leelas (1 July)
At suprabhatam (the author usually chants 'Om' twenty-one times on waking which is called Suprabhatam in Puttaparthy) and bhajans in the morning, I told Rita about the event and she told me how peaceful she and Radha felt after bhajans in this home last week. I thanked God for His Grace.

I came home early to clean up and noticed a piece of orange thread on the carpet. I asked Swami to send a bigger piece. Thanks for the thread but it was too miniscule. I felt absolutely positive of the Babas' presence. I saw the word 'Travel' unexpectedly on TV, a sign for the annual pilgrimage to Shirdi and Prashanti. I was waiting for a final sign from the Babas so that I could visit my country of birth yet again.

Dream (4 July)
The usual insomnia kept me awake. I eventually told the Babas that if they wanted me to do my job well let me sleep. I did fall asleep around 2.30 p.m. I had a very vivid dream indeed. I could see a bunch of us in a large room including Rita and Radha waiting for Swami to arrive. Then I saw myself with another group, telling them of my Shirdi and me. I had backed in a horse race and five straight races were won by me. The amount in question $80,000.10 summed up to the number 9. My dream ended. In the dream also I saw a picture of Jesus, betting on the horses with me. Way to go Jesus!

Shiva's Day (9 July)
After the readings, before going to work, it was quite dark. I noticed the Shiva Hologram near the entrance turn completely red, like it was on fire. There was no sunshine or light on. *Shiva on fire* on a Monday, looked absolutely beautiful. I stared. I loved God even more when such beauty was beheld. I prayed the rest of my life was filled with God, His Grace and His wonders.

11 July
I got on the train. The first thing I noticed in front of me etched in the seat ahead 'Jesus loves You'. I smiled, I love You too Jesus. I loved reading the book *The Wheel of Living* by Elizabeth Kubler

Rose. I could identify so much with her and her experiences, her spiritual ventures, if only I could have more and more moments of God as she had. Come on Shirdi Sai, Sathya Sai, Jesus Sai and all, please show me a few strong leelas. This was pure greed for the Divine and I didn't have guilt or a problem with being greedy for the Divine or Divinity.

12 July

I had a few whiffs during the day, thinking it to be udhi, but I didn't allow myself to get too excited. Before going home it was very strong, disappearing as suddenly as it had come. At Newtown Station I was approached by a Bengali colleague who asked me if I was wearing chandan (sandalwood); she said I was smelling of it. I said 'no', but realised then that that was what I was smelling during the day.

It was 5.30 a.m. It had rained heavily all night, but the first thing I saw on waking up was the beautiful morning star I see every morning, but this day there were two additional stars on either side. It was like looking straight at God in all Its glory. In this way He sweetly had started the day with me, my Shirdi Sai. I have mentioned earlier, I see Shirdi Sai in the morning and evening stars every day, in Surya too, in rainbows, the clouds, the moon, flowers, trees, fields, the birds, and nature in general.

A Challenge (18 July)

These sleepless nights were playing havoc with my mind, body and spirit. Most of last night I could safely say I had about an hour's sleep. I abused, was irate and annoyed at my lack of sleep. Eventually, I challenged the Babas stating they knew I was awake— 'You leave me during the night. Are You with me during the day? Show me, give me a sign, show me You are with me', I need this assurance from Baba and pestered Him many times to show me that He was with me, and that He was awake with me too. At around 5.30 a.m. a crescent-shaped moon, came shining through the bedroom window, lighting up the room, even though it was not a full moon, with beautiful stars all around it. It reminded me of the Beatles song 'Lucy in the sky with diamonds'. It was like another clarification to me, 'look I am awake to and with you'. It was so beautiful. My challenge was met. I calmed down, got out of bed and dressed for work when standing on the platform. I looked at the clear blue sky and suddenly saw the jet steam. Thank You Swami, I confirmed, You are omnipresent.

19 July

I was still waiting for Shirdi Sai to show me His omnipresence. He did. At lunch, I went to the Newsagent and saw an Indian/Australian newspaper, (which is never sold here but can be bought in Indian shops in Liverpool or other suburbs), which was rare in those parts, but was drawn to it so bought the same. On glancing through it, I was very happy indeed to see my beloved Shirdi Sai Baba and a news regarding His Sansthan in June issue.

August

Dream (22 August)

Lisa and Anna left on their holiday to London, Scotland, Ireland and Thailand. I prayed for a safe and joyous trip for them. I felt a bit down, even had a bit of a cry on the way home from work. Sometimes I felt very alone, forgetting that He was always with me, (human frailty). I had a restless night. I wished that with God's Grace the girls would be safe and would return safely. At last I slept. Prior to waking up I had a little dream about my beloved Baba of Shirdi. I saw, in my dream, I was with some people. Someone gave me a package which contained 'little things' but my excitement arose when I noticed the image of my Shirdi on all of them. I was very happy. Then I saw Shirin and I kept blessing her with the package as her baby was going to be born soon. My dream ended. I love You Baba.

September

Dream (3 September)

I had a very short dream early this morning. In a large room, pictures of the Babas were hanging all around. People were sitting around. A man came up to me and sort of latched himself on. I did not like the look of him. He was very forward and was behaving badly. I was getting a bit scared, even though I tried putting on a brave face. He then got even bolder and grabbed me around the waist. I looked at him straight in the eye and said, 'If you get any closer to me, you will have Him to deal with', pointing to a picture of Baba. The man looked at the picture and disappeared. Thank You Baba I feel safe, with You always with me.

Signs (19 September)

After one of the worst and tragic weeks affecting the entire world, particularly America, the wars, the Taliban, the tragedy of 9/11, there was an announcement that all Australians should cancel their trip to Asia or any place overseas as it was too dangerous to travel anywhere. I looked at the picture of Baba/Swami and said, 'I leave it to You Baba. Give me a sign if we should go to Parthy or stay here'. On opening the mail I received today, there was—

1. Baba's picture from Joy, a Sai devotee, who attends our weekly bhajans in Sydney;
2. Dulcie's (a retired secretary, whose job I now do) cheque for her sisters who happen to stay at Whitefield (she wanted me to deliver the cheque along with a food parcel to her sisters in Bangalore);
3. my itinerary; and
4. *Sanathana Sarathi.*

If these were not God's signs, I shall say no more, for I do not see them as coincidences. Swami/Baba was calling us and we were going, me being so very grateful for the signs from God in that awful time. Thank You.

20 September

The Blue Bird of Happiness appeared (Lord Krishna) after four years. I could not go to work as my tooth fell out. I went outside to put the garbage out and was delighted to see the little blue bird, (another sign). I remembered for the first time before going to Parthy, this little blue bird had appeared and danced on the fence. I told a friend about its beautiful blue colour and to see such an unreal bird in this backyard, where we only get mynahs and sparrows. She said it was Lord Krishna. To me it was another affirmation that we should travel. At noon aarti, I got a very brief wink from Shirdi and a rolling of the eyes. I was meant to stay home today. I also got a few whiffs of a beautiful aroma like jasmine when reading *Conversations with God* (Hislop). I was very thankful for this Divine Grace. Thy Will will be done.

The Trip (25 September)

My sweet mother came to the airport. Mum feared the war/terrorists and for my safety as all mothers do when their children are away. I arrived at Bangalore at 12.30 a.m. and was met by a new driver Bhupatti and Rahul the rogue who drove me to a hotel for the night. I could not stand it, the room was full of cockroaches, the bed was full of bed bugs. I was not feeling too well. My nose was bleeding, I had a bloated abdomen and was feeling very tired. I was then transferred to St. Marks where we (my Shirdi Sai and I) were remembered by all. It costed a fortune, but was worth it. I spent the morning shopping for my sister and the afternoon enjoying the sheer luxury of St. Marks. I had delicious vegetarian biryani and kulfi falooda. We loved the place and we savoured the food. There was an earthquake while we were flying into Bangalore last night. Thank God, I was with the Godly team, up in the sky and not on earth yet.

28 September
First darshan of our beloved Swami was not too far away, so I got a good view. He looked a bit skinny and very frail, but oh so charming! The tears came along with the desires. After darshan I was surprised to see a new shopping complex with three levels and a beautiful book shop. I couldn't wait to buy any new book. The electricity failed, the computer failed, so they had to resort to the old slate calculations, while we had to grit our teeth, wait in line patiently while Swami tested our saburi. It was worth it, in the end I was given a flower along with my books. I stayed outside for the afternoon bhajans and had darshan of Swami walking into His home. I loved watching from there, got a good view and could avoid the crowds inside the Sai Kulwant Hall.

Bleeding Stops (29 September)
Before going to darshan this morning, I noticed I was bleeding (like a normal lady during her menses). I was rather surprised as I had had a total hysterectomy twenty years ago and have since never had a bleed. I put this down to tiredness, and after a shower, continued on my way to darshan, wearing something for protection. Not giving the bleeding any more thought, I got to the sixth row and had beautiful darshan of Swami. Swami stood on the platform and He really looked so serene and lovely. He blessed us all with His beautiful darshan. The weather was awful. It was raining heavily and the roads were in a mess. After darshan I ran into the 'Sai Sadan' only to find that the bleeding had started all over again. Just prior to

trying to get into my room in a hurry, I noticed a large door across from mine, on the sixth floor in 'Sai Sadan' with carvings of Shirdi Sai and Sathya Sai, with bhajans being sung inside and could hear that there was much clapping. I found out from the boy that it was a puja/bhajan hall with a suite attached, which was being leased by a Japanese family. I was still bleeding, so I put some vibhuti on my stomach and prayed that whatever was ailing me be removed, not wanting to go to a doctor and at the same time getting afraid of this. The bleeding suddenly stopped. I still don't know why or for what reason this happened, but I was fine after that.

The Fan Man (30 September)
I missed going to Shirdi on this trip and felt quite miserable about that decision. After another beautiful darshan I rang Mum. It was good to hear her voice and that all was okay at home. I went shopping and the caretaker who looked after the cushions and the fans outside the shopping complex, shook his head in despair when he saw Shirdi Sai and the Lotus Feet of Swami glued to my plastic hand fan. He said this was insulting and should not be there. I told him they had been there for four years and would only come off *if They wanted to.* He looked very angry with me. I attended a lecture given by Anil Kumar. His voice was so loud, that a loudspeaker was not necessary. I sat outside and listened, it was softer on the ears.

October

Car Darshan (1 October)
There were too many people here as was expected. I did some seva in the kitchen today, and got to repeat *Sai Ram* often which I loved. I went back for bhajans and after the same I went to get my slippers, but there was a huge crowd with everybody pushing. It was pouring, and the place was slippery and muddy. I eventually found the slippers. I was heading towards the shops when I noticed everybody standing in a queue even though it was pouring heavily. I realised they were waiting for Swami to come. True enough, I saw the car, I stopped, the car was going very slowly I stood on my toes and had the most beautiful darshan of a very happy smiling Swami. I forgot myself and shouted 'I love You Swami'. I was very happy.

Shirdi Sai (2 October)

I had to go back to the cloakroom after trying to get into line, to return the umbrella and purse as they were no longer allowed to be taken into the Sai Kulwant Hall. I got a back row but sat against the wall. Even then I got a good darshan of Swami. After darshan I walked in the garden and I was feeling very sorry to see the sad plight of my beloved Shirdi Sai's stone slab in the garden. He should have had an umbrella over Him. I put a rose before Him but half an hour later it was not there. (He had given it to somebody else.) I bought You flowers and You gave it away! The stone slab needed to be repaired and repainted. I saw the gardener a few times but did not complain. I left this at the Lotus Feet of Swami for Him to look after my Shirdi Sai in the garden. Before leaving on this trip, I invited Shirdi Sai to accompany me through the trip and also through my life. I cannot explain how many times my beloved Shirdi Sai gave me His beautiful darshan that day in some form or the other.

The Dogs (3 October)

The dogs were in a putrid state here, full of mange, thin, they howled in pain and I asked myself why was it that they being right under Swami's care yet were in such a poor state. After darshan, I was walking to the canteen and I saw a boy kick one of the dogs. My anger came to the fore but I held my tongue. I had an aversion to bullies, more especially the ones who hurt helpless animals. A lady walking beside me came to me and said, 'I just saw your face, I feel the same way. Why do these dogs have to suffer like this?' I stated, 'I know it is their karma, but shouldn't Swami or at least man take care of these poor animals, spay them so that they cannot keep on producing pariahs who end up the same way as they do?' We both were very sad. She was from Holland. I walked towards the daabwallah (who sold coconuts) and to my dismay saw two puppies, and one of them looked extremely ill and weak and could barely stand or raise his little head. Then a European gentleman got the puppies together and started to pray over them placing his hands on them ever so gently and closing his eyes in deep prayer. I was very touched and started to cry. I was having a malai daab when the pup's mother stood beside me, so I gave her the malai, she relished it, I was hoping that everyone else would do the same.

God bless and care for these helpless creatures, why should they have to suffer? Please, no thoughts on karma here.

5 October

I couldn't wait to get to darshan. I wanted so much to be at the Lotus Feet for my fifty-fifth birthday which was on that day. I was happy to have been in the fifth line. I thought of going to the side instead of against the wall, but a Seva Dal member looked at me as I was heading towards the back row and said, 'Madam, sit here – first row'. It was like the seat had been reserved for me. With a big smile on my face and in my heart, I quietly thanked Swami for His Grace (and Shirdi Sai too). After the interviews were over and an overall beautiful darshan, Swami glided by smiling so sweetly. Thank You Swami. I felt very blessed. I went back to the room after breakfast and all the hotel staff were standing in line, from the Manager to the boy and said 'Happy Birthday Memsahib'. The cleaner must have seen the cards on my table. I had to shed a tear. I rang Mum. She said 'Happy Birthday' and 'God Bless You'. I replied, 'He did, this morning, I got line 1'. We both laughed.

Line 1 (6 October)

I got the second line but I decided to go to where I was yesterday, and the same place was vacant. In all the four years that I have been to Parthy, I have never had such close and beautiful darshan from Swami. Though it was very uncomfortable to sit for four hours, in the end to see Swami glide by ever so gently, was truly worth every ache. The weather was not so good. I sat outside after darshan and cried at the beautiful bhajans sung. After bhajans/darshan, Swami was walking back and a Seva Dal member tried to hold an umbrella up for Swami, but He refused it preferring to be like all the devotees without umbrellas and walk in the rain. I had a good laugh.

Line 1 (7 October)

Well, things always happen in 3s. Again I got line 2 but that first row seat was yet again waiting for me. I declined though (as you cannot leave the hall until Swami goes back to his room after bhajans). I could not sit for so long with my arthritic knees, so I sat in the second row instead, as I also needed to have breakfast, (Shirdi Sai never likes one to go hungry). My seat was looked after by a beautiful lady till my return. As usual, Swami gave excellent and long darshan, particularly on the stage. There was some festival. All the students were given shiny apples/oranges by Swami. They walked round the mandir chanting the Vedas and headed towards the Chitravarthi River. Then Swami's car made a sudden and swift appearance in front of Sai Kulwant Hall, drove Swami off, while we waited for His return. Darshan was lovely and long. I went to a lecture and was very impressed by the lecturer named Tulsidas. He spoke so softly so clearly and so lovingly of Swami, with a touch of humour. It was great!

Bhajans Hall (8 October)

It was my last day at Parthy. I felt as though I have not completed my trip as I missed Shirdi very much. I would try not to bypass it again, and wished with all my heart that I could go to Shirdi before the year ends. I went back to the hotel to pack. The Japs had left and I asked the boy if I could take a peak into the bhajan room while he cleaned. I was shocked when I entered. There was a beautiful raised puja area, two magnificent pictures of the Babas and it was spotless. I couldn't help but run up and kiss the feet. Then I noticed the suite. I wished I could have extended my stay, but for the next time I knew where I would be staying, God willing, in the suite in the puja room at Sai Sadan. Won't that just be Divine?

Last Darshan—Paduka Day (9 October)

I rushed to darshan in the pouring rain. The whole Hall was filled to the very end, me being last. It was past 7.30 a.m., Swami hadn't come in, I was panicking as the driver was coming at 9.00 to drive us back to Bangalore. At 7.45, I got up, rushed out of the Hall and had to keep going, even though it was pouring with rain, to get back to the hotel before the driver arrived. Swami had still not arrived. Heading towards the steps when something made me turn around outside at the very end of Sai Kulwant Hall, near the grille, I got a perfect view of Swami on stage. It was like Swami giving me my last darshan. I stood there for about five minutes. I was very grateful and happy, as I didn't want to leave without the last darshan of Swami. On the way to Bangalore, I stopped to farewell my darling Shirdi Sai, noting a big Jain Temple. I must visit it one day.

Shirdi Sai's Spirit/Shiva Tree (10 October)

I arrived at Thayiammas Ashram, Bangalore. I was glad to see three mandirs of Shirdi there. The pujari was doing a puja when we entered. I was so very happy to see my Shirdi Sai. I felt like I was in Shirdi. (He had answered me by bringing me to this place, knowing how much I missed going to Shirdi.) We entered the second temple where there was a dark murti of Baba along with some old pictures, also of the lady who passed away in 1996 at the age of 112. I did another puja then and was onto the third temple where there was a Shirdi murti, wearing a beautiful flower in his left ear covered with a shawl. The pujari did the puja. I then lifted Shirdi's shawl to put some dakshina into Baba's tumrel. I next saw a ghostly apparition or spirit or I don't really know what to call it, come out of Baba's statue (it reminded me of Casper the friendly ghost), which placed the flower which was in His ear, into my hand. The pujari looked so shocked, he yelled to the driver and told Him what had happened as he had also witnessed this. The spirit put the flower in my hand. I was in bliss supreme, but was also extremely shocked but unafraid. After darshan, we were going to the car when the pujari called us back and took us to a tree called The Shiva Tree. He made the driver climb up and remove a flower for me. When the driver gave me the flower I realised why it was called the Shiva Tree. The flower opened up and it looked like a serpent behind a lingam like Shiva.

11 October

I visited a priest and old friend briefly. He was a delight, but I had to continue to Mysore with a new driver who was a speed freak. I was very frightened and uncomfortable with him. Halagappa as usual was on his campcot. I forced him to open the temple. He gave me two packets of vibhuti, only I wanted to see the padukas and Shirdi Sai's murti, so he got a guide to take me down to the Cauvery River where a beautiful big picture of Swami was hung outside on the balcony looking across the river. I worshipped my Shirdi's padukas, went into the new mandir upstairs where I was allowed into Swami's new bedroom, the new meditation room/temple with beautiful statues of Jesus, Buddha and my Beloved in a special dome-like area.

****

23 October

I had a dream where I was standing with a few people. I saw Swami walking towards me. As He got closer He put His hands, covering

His face, smiling mischievously. He went away. I went to the altar where a flower fell at my feet, but I did not pick it up. I moved away and cursed myself for not having picked up the flower. Then I saw Swami coming towards me again. He was very near me and I could hear Him say, 'Come Come' while He moved His hand, gesturing me towards Him. He looked very young. The dream ended.

Darshan (26 October)
I was flooded with work with one of the staff specialists dictating and amending the same letter over and over again. I was amazed at how 'unruffled' I was, patient and calm. He was holding up all the other work I had to do, a test here for me, but I passed it but staying calm. I kept repeating to myself '*Om Sai Ram*'. Everything went well, eventually he signed the letter, went back to his work happy and so was I. On the way home, I was berating Shirdi for not showing Himself to me. I stood all the way to Glenfield, reading all the graffiti on the train, noticed one that stood out—the word 'Sufi'. Thank You Baba, You showed Yourself in the Sufi form.

What a Day (28 October)
I went to bhajans, then food shopping. The trolley was laden, fearful at the finish thinking the bill would be about $200 but it was only $125 the exact amount I had. When I got home, I received a call from Kala saying Colin/Shanti (a very interesting family, very close to Babas with many experiences between them) were going to the Indian Fair in Liverpool, then on to the Shirdi Temple at Strathfield. The heart raced, such joy, such bliss, such grace! We didn't stay too long at the fair. I bought some more food at the fair (I had been food shopping earlier as mentioned above) and then we drove on to Strathfield. Our Baba was so very kind, it being a very special day as they were celebrating Durga Puja. I went to the temple, and saw my most Loved. I spoke to Mr Rao who told me a miracle took place there two weeks ago when a fifteen-month-old baby who could not even stand, was brought to the temple and he ran to Baba's murti. There was more grace—the kakad aarti started, at 4.00p.m. There was only about fourteen of us in the temple. We took it in turn to do the aarti (three times each). At the end of the aarti it was like being in Shirdi they played the closing of the aarti from the Samadhi Mandir in Shirdi. The crowd started swelling and we went into a large tent where ghazals were sung. Around 7.30

p.m. I was really tired, so was Kala, but very happy. Thank You the Babas. We ate beautiful and tasty dinner (prasad) and then went home. Kala loaned me the Shirdi Baba video. I put the video in, it was about 9.30 p.m. I was very tired but determined to see my Deva, before retiring for the night. The video would not work, I tried again and asked Baba to make it work, He did, it worked. Thank you Colin, Shanti, Chantelle for your kindness, in driving us to all these lovely places today and then driving us back home. Here was an interesting family, very close to Swami and Shirdi Sai, Chantelle their beautiful daughter, had quite a few experiences herself with the Babas as did her mother Shanti. Colin has since tragically passed away. May his soul be peaceful.

November

Dream (5 November)

I cannot quite remember all of the dream, but very clearly remember seeing Swami, a young Swami, wearing a type of heavy navy uniform with ornate gold buttons and tassels. A man was talking to Swami and Swami gave him thirteen little plastic plates and cups and I was watching and explaining what Swami was doing, to someone there. The dream ended.

Melbourne Cup (6 November)

Ethereal won; I had this nagging feeling it would, but did not place a bet on the Totalizator Agency Board (where people place bets for horse racing, etc.) although I won the sweep at work—$12 for $1. Then it hit me, the dream I had last night—Swami's strange outfit—a jockey suit—the thirteen cups—number thirteen won the cup and the jockey wore navy blue/white. According to Radha there was a message in this dream—no more gambling.

Akhanda Bhajans (10 November)

I went to attend Akhanda bhajans with Kala and Henry (this was held once a year and bhajans are sung from 6 p.m. to 6 p.m. the next evening, i.e., 24 hours). The picture of Swami was beautiful, and so real. The bhajans were lovely and Swami's darshan was very blissful. Towards the end I saw Swami's forehead just turned white. The rest of the picture was normal. It looked like it was standing out saying 'the mind, the brain, the wisdom' this was the seat. I felt there was another message for me—saburi.

Dream (13 November)

I had an awful night. It was my fault, I ate too many chocolates. I must have had about two hours sleep. It was my fault for being greedy and sugar does keep one up at night. I had a very short dream early in the morning. I had more of a nap than a sleep, hence the dream was short. I saw a lorry with a man doing his puja on it. As the lorry passed by, I got a glimpse of Baba, which made me happy. I also got the darshan of Ganapati and a few other gods/goddesses. I was happy. My dream came to an end. I was even happier to have got my first e-mail from the Shirdi temple in Strathfield, which provided me with the timings of aarti and experiences occurring at the temple.

A Very Strange Dream (17 November)

Just before rising, around 5 a.m. in my dream I saw that I was travelling alone to the city. It was very dark and dismal, and there was nobody around. On getting off the bus I was glad to see my family friends. They were determined to buy this big house. Then I saw Prasanna and Joy (Sai devotees from our bhajan group) with what looked like little pots of vibhuti in their hands, which they offered me and I took some. I was then in a large house. There were two Indian men—one handed me an odd looking button and asked me to find the other one which had fallen off. I couldn't find it.

Next I saw Shirin with an enormous plate of rice which she was eating. I asked her if she was pregnant, she said she thought so. Someone told me my goods were arriving, I got a bit scared as I had no money to pay for them but was also excited.

Then I saw a very large hall, with some members of our bhajan group. There was a very slim, handsome pujari who looked very similar to a young Jesus/Shirdi Sai and was very calm and serene looking. Just prior to the starting of the puja, I looked at my left palm and an *Om* appeared on it. I asked the pujari what it meant. He said something to me, but I never understood him. Then a swastika appeared on my hand, I showed it to Joy who was sitting next to me, but she was disinterested. Then my whole left palm was covered with red writing. Most distinct from all the other words was Baba Baba Baba. I have never looked or been more excited. The dream ended here. I got up excited. I prayed that it was a good message from Baba. The pujari was wearing a long white robe.

18 November

Alika rang me to explain 'the dream'. The swastika is perhaps the oldest symbol on earth, standing for 'peace' in the Hindu scriptures (Shirdi Temple also have this symbol in them). The white robed man was Jesus. She felt like Jesus/Shirdi Sai/Swami were all with me. I myself was still not very clear about this dream although I felt it was a very significant and progressive dream in my heart.

The Cake Story (22 November)

I worked till 1.00 and went into Town Hall to buy the ingredients for the vegetarian Fruit Cake. I was very excited as the recipe was so very simple and the cake mixture just sort of 'fell into place' so easily. I didn't even have to double up the quantity, as it took up the whole large pan. This was for Swami's birthday.

Then the fun started. I turned the oven on and the gas would not light. I could not believe my eyes. I started laughing and told Swami that the joke was over now, the cake had to be baked, that I was growing anxious. After about ten minutes Swami decided to stop His prank, the oven lit up. I loved the leela Swami, I had a good laugh. After all the drama, the cake was delicious.

23 November

A very Happy Birthday to You dearest Swami.

Another Cake Story (24 November)

The fruit cake baked on Thursday was huge but took only an hour to bake (after the oven leela drama). I woke up early to bake the chocolate cake for tomorrow. It was simple enough but small. Baking time stated in the recipe was one and a half hours. I put it in the oven at 9.10 a.m. It was only done at 12.15 p.m. It took three hours to bake a mini cake! Thanks Swami, another prank of Yours!

I was being picked up at 1.15p.m., so I could not ice the cake but decided to put some pecans on top and a candle. At about 12.45p.m. (the cake was cool), I placed a small candle on the top and while sticking the pecans in, I noticed the candle had disappeared from the top, just a bit of wick left sticking out. I had a very hearty laugh, it being hilarious to see just the wick. Lovely leela! Three hours to bake and a disappearing candle! Eventually on returning from Swami's beautiful birthday at Prairievale where I was given heaps of coloured vibhuti packets, two roses, hugs and kisses from friends, a picture of Swami, I placed a big round candle on the chocolate cake for our bhajans to be held the next day.

Vibhuti Dream (25 November)
In my dream I saw ourselves at bhajans. I was a bit distressed. They had kept an event from me. Lisa and myself were in another hall. Lisa was just about to leave when a pujari, tall, lean and very handsome entered the hall wearing a loincloth. He put vibhuti on my forehead. Lisa came running back and just in time. I also got vibhuti placed on her forehead.

December

Beautiful Leelas and Bliss (12 December)
Early this morning, I was just voicing to myself that there were no leelas, no smell of vibhuti, no dreams, no darshan, sparshan and *sambhashan,* etc., and I felt quite sad. I went to bhajans, before going into the hall. Kala and I were sitting in the car waiting for all the other Sai devotees to arrive for bhajans. The sky was a beautiful blue and then I saw the longest jet steam. Swami was flying over, which delighted me—after a long time seeing Swami by the sign from Swami—the jet steam.

Then I went in for bhajans. The altar was laden with my favourite flowers gardenias, of all sizes and all were beautiful and fragrant. Mrs Nair who had brought all the gardenias from her home, told me to take *all the flowers after* bhajans, which made me very happy indeed, as we normally share the flowers between all of us. Just before bhajans started, I was standing at the Swami picture. I looked at Swami and said, 'I hope You don't think I'm being greedy, but Mrs Nair told me to take all the gardenias. If You think this is okay, please drop a flower from above Your picture'. This was my first ever immediate leela. A few flowers fell, I was aghast. I had to run over to tell Radha. Thank You Swami, please don't stop, please permit me Your Grace and Your experiences for life.

At home I did nama japa for Shirdi Baba and then went to the puja room to do afternoon aarti. Shirdi Sai was there in the flesh. His face looked like it had blood in its veins, His eyes moved. He looked so real. I was so very grateful for a very beautiful darshan.

16 December

I was very happy that we managed to get a simple but beautiful manger for Christmas. On doing the morning Jesus prayer for a brief time, a definite 'Light' shone from the Holy Face of Jesus. I prayed for a darshan and thanked Him for the beautiful crib and manger. I decided to decorate it lovingly. I said to myself, 'As You were born there, so let's make it cosy and warm for You this Christmas, away in the manger.'

29 December

Jagind and Alika, friends of mine, was coming for dinner tonight. I pestered Shirdi Sai to make His presence felt or to show me that He was with us. Also, I got dressed and waited. They were meant to come at 6.30 p.m. but didn't arrive till 8. While waiting I decided to glance through the *Angel Book* given to me by Lisa for Christmas. I just opened a page and the first words were 'I Am Always With You'. I knew my beloved Shirdi Sai had affirmed my request yet again in His own way. I love Him so much and didn't He know it? Thank You my Baba, leave me never, love me ever.

2002

January

Dream (3 January)

I was thrilled—it was my first dream in the first week of the year. I saw Sharon, Lisa and myself in a big dark room filled with different-shaped candles. We lit the first candle. It was Lord Ganesh, after burning a while I noticed the Ganesh candle had turned into Shirdi Sai, wearing His scarf. Naturally, I was beaming. I went along explaining to Sharon and Lisa, as we lit each large candle, who the different Gods were, but they all appeared to turn into Shirdi Sai. There was a very large statue, that too was lit. I commented it would glow for hours. Then there was another, but the wick would not burn because it was encased/tangled in a lot of thread. I told Lisa to remove the threads, as Baba was protecting us, if we lit that one, the threads would cause a fire. His kindness and protection was evident, even in a dream. Thank You my Beloved. Then I saw myself with Kala and Henry in two very quaint cars. We were driving through a very dangerous field of rocks. We were coming to a crossroad and taking a wrong turn, and were heading into oncoming traffic, but the other cars were far enough for us to turn safely around to head in the right direction. The dream ended. This did actually happen to us on Deepavali last year. After dinner at a friend's home, Henry, Kala and I were driving home only to discover (it was very dark) that we were on a one-way street, going the wrong way. Thankfully, there was no traffic at that time of the night. Henry quickly made a u-turn and we drove home safely. *Sai Ram.*

Utter Bliss (26 January)

I cleaned the puja room today with Baba's permission. I put one of the Shirdi shawls on the altar and the other one was going to grace the bed. At noon aarti, after many months, I got 'the white light' radiating from Shirdi Sai's picture on the altar. I was mesmerised. His lips became white, it was like He was trying to say something to me. The eyes moved, the face turned to flesh and my Baba was with me. I could only say very humbly Thank You my beloved Baba for such beautiful blissful grace and it lasted for about seven to nine minutes. I love You my God. During the afternoon aarti, my heart, I thought actually stopped beating. It happened again. There was no light but Shirdi Sai's eyes actually moved from side to side. I could not believe my eyes. I stood perfectly still, like I had held my breath. I could feel His presence and I was very close to Him. I know that He was here with me.

February

Bedroom Bliss (2 February)

I finished all the prayers and was at the last picture of Swami hanging above the bed. I was amazed. For the first time I got darshan of Swami from this picture. I had to blink twice to see if my eyes were not playing tricks on me. They were not. I moved directly in front of the picture and was very happy to see the White Light, though faint, cover Swami's beautiful thick black hair and move on to His face. It was very beautiful indeed! Humble *pranaams* Swami.

God's Grace (12 February)

I complained to the Babas on opening the fridge and finding it empty, not even a grain of rice. This evening the fridge was full. Shirin's mother had cooked for me. Thanks to the grace of the Babas. *Koti koti pranaams* Baba/Swami, and thank you Shirin's dear mother, I love you and your food.

The Cup (15 February)

I had resorted to taking the steroids for my very swollen face, but after much discussion with the Baba, should I or should I not, one of the medicine cups that I drank vibhuti from had disappeared. I even looked in the garbage bin, but could not find it. Okay Babas I got the message and will take the medicine although if it were my will, I would have stuck with the udhi/vibhuti. I just do not feel happy taking medication, it is rather a contradiction for me, I have surrendered to Shirdi Sai, is He not meant to be looking after my health too?

Dream (16 February)

I had a short dream. I saw I was with the bhajan group, and could see Radha/Jesu and myself conversing. Jesu said to me 'God wants you to...' I awoke. I realised that I will have to wait for God to tell me what He wants me to.

March

1 March

I read an excellent book called *One Souls Journey* by Leni Matlin. It would have been great if I could meet the author.

How Can You Mend a Broken Heart (2 March)

I didn't look in the mailbox yesterday as I got home from the dentist after being anaesthetised. I was feeling very groggy today but took a walk to Leumeah to get some bread/milk. On returning, I opened the mail box to find to my extreme joy, an envelope from Shirdi. It was a receipt and a letter of thanks for a miniscule donation sent. They also stated: 'Enclosed is udhi.' I was thrilled as I had only washed the vibhuti/udhi container a little while ago as it was empty. This was like a true gift from God. I searched the letter and envelope but there was no udhi. My heart sank, I was very sad and disappointed. At noon aarti, after many weeks and months, I got a beautiful darshan from Swami. It was not very long but enough for me to realise that the Babas had heard me. Was it any wonder my lips were an enigma to the medical people? The doctors were actually confounded as to what was ailing my lips; they were blue and very swollen and no one knew why; I did.

Dream (6 March)

It was very early this morning before waking up that I had a dream. I saw a remote village with a large house. Everyone was getting ready for Anjali's 21st birthday. Dad and Mum were there. There were many people, and it was a strange scenery. Mum looked through a large glass window and pointed saying 'There's Sai Baba'. She was right, the orange robe, the silent guest walking in the distance. My dream ended. In reality Anjali's 21st birthday was the day before. I was very happy to get Swami's darshan at Anjali's party even though it was in dream form and four days prior to the 21st party held for Anjali.

10 March

Anjali's 21st birthday party was beautiful. The hall was full of people who gave so much love. Even I felt very loved and indeed very happy to be a guest of the Kottieth family, whom I loved dearly. God bless and guide you Anjali. Swami was in attendance as per the dream I had on 6 March.

Mahashivaratri (12 March)

Mahashivaratri is Shiva's night. I love Shiva, so even more reason to go to Shivaratri as Shirdi Sai is meant to be the reincarnation of Lord Shiva. Therefore, I doubly love this day, it always feels like a magical day to me, even though I do not know too much about it. I did the normal prayers with a few extras to Shiva. At noon aarti I noticed the light very faint, moving from picture to picture—from Shirdi Sai to Swami to Vishnu to Hanuman getting stronger till it got to Shiva's statue then it got very strong. When it fell on the main altar, Shirdi Sai first closed His left eye. Then the beautiful darshan that He gave was strong/beautiful/blissful and ever loving. Humbly, thank You my beloved Sai.

Festivities at Bonnyrigg were beautiful, the bhajans were delirious so was I particularly during the recitation of *Om Namah Shivaya* for 108 times. I got the most glorious smell of marigolds, the aroma being strong and lasting till the 108th mantra. I knew my Shiva/Shirdi was there. I could have reached the targeted recitation of *Namah Shivayas* for 10,008 times. This was Baba/Shiva letting me know that I had reached my target of 10,008 *Namah Shivayas* by sending me the fragrance of flowers that were not even in the hall at the time. No one else got the smell of the flowers, I did ask a few people there if they had smelt flowers, they all nodded 'No'. During the course of the bhajans I requested Swami,'The minute you materialise a lingam today, let me get a knot in my stomach'. I got home at 1 a.m. At 1.15 I got a severe pain in the stomach. I bent over. It was so sharp. Then I realised immediately my request to Swami. *Om Namah Shivaya. Koti koti pranaams* Shirdi Sai for the beautiful noon darshan and *koti koti pranaams* Swami for the twitch.

Dreams

26 March

What a dream it was! Before going to bed last night I wrote a letter to Baba about life. I had a dream at about 3.30 a.m. I was talking to someone. I was very panicked being late for work. I tried phoning many times, but could not remember the right number, and in sheer desperation, I kept hitting the buttons furiously. Lisa was standing near me. I was telling her to get the office number. We seemed to be getting all the other numbers but the right one. Then I saw the room filled with patients, me being the controller in the scene, telling the patients where to go, what to do even what medications to take, except for a Korean boy. I am ashamed to admit my bad behaviour in a dream, and eventually I had thrown the boy out of the house. Then I was back to the phone, when suddenly out of the floor appeared Swami. Swami was standing very near. Then I saw Mum and Lisa staring at Swami. I tried to push them closer to Swami, and then I awoke. I was very thankful and grateful for Swami's warmth.

I popped into the church today, remembering it was Holy week. I asked Jesus to give me a bit of Palm, as it had been Palm Sunday the day before (according to the Gospel [the Bible] of John 11.12, just before Crucification, Jesus on entering Jerusalem was greeted by all with the waving of palms). In the Christian calendar to date, a week before Easter Sunday every year, pieces of palms are distributed to the people at mass. On entering the church, on the table there was a mini bit of palm, with a thorn in it. Thank You Jesus and thank You also for the Easter eggs.

****

29 March

It was a very strange dream. I was in the coffin position, with a pujari standing near. I could hear the word 'Shirdi'. The pujari gave me a handful of mud which I put into my mouth, it being very thick, coarse and grainy and I could not swallow it. I heard the word 'Shirdi' again. Water was then given to me by the pujari. I asked him if it was Shirdi water and he nodded. This brought me to the end of my bizarre dream.

Bhajans (31 March)

Bhajans and Study Circle was held at our home today with the Babas' blessings and attended by God and His party, along with Kala, Henry, Rita, Radha, Anjali, Archi, Rohit, Prasanna, Ashwin, Harish, Manju, Savita's mother, Colin, Shanthi, Chantelle, Rajesh, Shirin, Mrs Nair and grandchild, Jesu, Indrani and daughter, Saroj and husband. I noticed a spot of vibhuti on Swami's third eye area, briefly. After bhajans, Shirdi on the wall gave three flashes. It looked like miniature lightning. Then the image became so life-like, ghostly but visible. I thought Shirdi Sai was going to jump off the wall.

I asked for another sign that I am not deluding myself. *Allah aacha karega* (Allah will do good).

April

Nishtha and Saburi (20 April)

After a 'trying and testing' week that had just gone by, God showed His Divine Grace in abundance as the following events revealed:

My upgrade in position at work was supported by the Board, from a 3 to a 5.

On awakening this morning, I prayed—I hoped that I would meet an angel today. I was heard. It came in the form of Karl, who fixed my gas leak and charged me nothing. It is very expensive here to call for plumbers at home for help and none gives anything free.

May

10 May

Last night I was glancing through the *Women's Weekly Magazine* one more time before disposing it off. A short story of Rolf Harris (an Australian icon in the field of entertainment), caught my eye. I was about to go past it yet again but read on looking at a picture of him and his wife. I looked again and there in the background was a picture of our beloved Swami in Rolf's studio. I felt great joy on obtaining the darshan of Swami, even from a magazine. Thanks Swami.

Support (11 May)

At prayer this morning, I prayed, 'God help me to help others'. 'I stand before Thy Lotus Feet oh Lord, please look after Lisa and me,

I beg Your support dear Lord.' After that, like I did every week, I pulled an Angel Card asking God to guide and help me through the week. The card I pulled out was 'support' (Sai support!).

Dream (23 May)

I dreamt around 4 or 5.30 a.m. I was walking up many flights of stairs, of a very tall building. I stopped. Instead of continuing up the stairs, I took a wrong turn. There were no more stairs, just a long dark sheer drop. Before I fell down the pit, I managed to grab a rail and hung on to get my balance again and started ascending. I got to the top and saw a huge glass pane. On looking out, the sky was a beautiful blue with fluffy white clouds, even though the sun was shining brightly. Each cloud formed an 'Om'. The whole sky was filled with 'Oms'. I was delighted at this breathtaking spectacle. The dream ended.

June

2 June

On the way to bhajans I noticed a book in the car given to Kala for the library called: *God Medical Practice and Healing*. I felt very drawn to the book and even though I had borrowed three books, the day before, I borrowed this one too. It was all about being healed by God instead of modern medicine. It seemed like an affirmation to me to trust the Lord. I decided against the hypebaric treatment that I was to undergo for the gums and teeth. I would unfortunately have to continue with the dentists though. The book borrowed might be a source of guidance for me as to what was the next step.

Amazing Grace (3 June)

Manouri returned from seeing Swami today in Parthy. She looked radiant and peaceful. She saw Swami at Whitefield for Visak – Buddha's birthday – and gave me the joyous news that Swami had taken my letter. She explained that she, her mother and a friend (who was visiting Swami for the first time) got the first row. Her friend was holding the letter, being a first timer. Swami passed by as she graciously held it in her lap when Swami walked on. Swami then turned around, walked back to the lady (the friend with the letter) and took the letter from her hand. Manouri and her mother were stunned onlookers, so was I when told. Thank You dear Swami, You know how very much this is appreciated.

5 June

I had no sleep at all. I was as usual complaining to the Babas that they would have to get me through the day. Even though I was extremely tired, the day turned out to be one filled with God's amazing grace, yet again.

- On the way to the station I saw a double jet steam, the Babas showing that they were with me.
- I read *Sai Liberator* and kept asking the Babas to give me further evidence that they were with me. They did, which I will explain in the following page.
- I got into the train carriage, very tired, but I was glad to see that the carriage number added to nine.
- I got off the train at Redfern, and was approached by a man saying he repeatedly read Sai books. 'Yes, Yes, Yes, I am one of His,' was my reply. He was from Malaysia, had only been here for four months with his family, and had attended bhajans at Casula.
- I was very hungry, before I got to work but had no money to buy anything. On my desk was a muffin made by Karen. Thank You Babas. I was no longer hungry.

I went to Westmead where I was examined and was told that some teeth would have to be removed, though the lower gums had slightly improved. I told the doctor that I preferred to wait and manage the teeth with God's help. He stated it was my choice. He then proceeded to remove two fillings which were already there, with no anaesthetic local or otherwise, no needles. He tugged and tugged, while I prayed and prayed. At one stage he stated, 'The Indian God with many hands—Lord Ganesha is hearing your prayers'. I laughed. After an hour of intense pulling and tugging, cleaning with corticosteroids for the abscess, it was over. After the ordeal during which I had continuously chanted *Om Sai Shri Sai Jai Jai Sai* (it being a Thursday), I vowed to Shirdi Sai that I would repeat the *Om Sai* 1008 times in thankfulness for no pain. Thank You God for Your amazing and welcome grace.

7 June

I saw the cardiologist. What a sweet man he was, so caring and so thorough. I have never felt so 'looked after' by a doctor. After being with him for an hour, the heart seemed to be okay but he would like me to have a few tests, i.e., cholesterol, triglycerides, doppler, etc., to be sure. He also affirmed to me for some reason, about my decision regarding hyperbaric treatment. I should not have hyperbaric treatment. It was like a direction from the Babas. After all, he stated what guarantees are there of the abscesses in the mouth not returning even after such treatment. The doctor was very shocked at my having had (his words) one of the worst cancers and that too at such an early age. He was very sympathetic and before I left he said, 'Don't worry everything will be all right. We will look after you'. Again I felt this was a message from the Babas.

On the way home, after seeing the doctor, I sat near a very old, well-dressed and frail-looking man with the most beautiful big blue eyes and a lovely smell about him. I kept wondering to myself, 'He looks so feeble and yet he is travelling so far by himself on a train'. We kept glancing at each other, and smiling, and I couldn't help but admire his beautiful big blue eyes. He would have been in his 80s or 90s. He reminded me of my Shirdi Sai, having similar eyes. I felt very happy thinking to myself, 'If this is Shirdi Sai, He will get off at Leumeah with me'. He did.

It was 1.17 a.m. I had started reading *Shubara Marga Shirdi Sai Baba*. This chapter was about 'Nayana Deeksha'—the intensity of the look from Baba's eyes. This was not a crazy notion or ego for that matter, but if I saw a stranger with penetrating eyes, looking at me, I always knew it was my Shirdi Sai, this had also been clarified by Him on occasions.

Grace, Grace and More Grace (10 June)

I went to the Shirdi Temple at Strathfield in time for kakad aarti which started at 9.30 a.m. The pujari recognised me, smiled and gave me a booklet but I did not understand the words, so I just gazed at my beloved Babas' beautifully adorned murti, wearing a beautiful garland of roses. I prayed for one rose from the garland. The pujari asked me to do aarti. I was feeling shy. There were so many people. The inner voice said, 'Ego not shy'. A lady then approached me and took me to the altar where I had to do the aarti. I noticed a beautiful black and white picture of Shirdi Sai, His full face, which I had not seen before. I was captivated as it was a full picture of Baba's face. After aarti, the lady asked me to wait for prasad. A man was distributing pieces of sliced fruit to all; when he came to me he gave me a whole apple (Baba feeds me). I could not stop smiling. I asked the pujari about the picture. He was going to e-mail the same to me. I was putting on the shoes ready to walk all the long way to the station, when I noticed that the man who distributed the fruits was ready to dispose off the roses that was on Baba's murti. I called out to him, as I wanted one rose from it. He gave me the whole heavy garland, much to my delight. He stated the garland was very heavy and he would put it in my car. I told him I did not have a car. He put the heavy garland into my bag and drove me to the station himself. His name was Raj.

11 June

I have never eaten an apple in many years, as I cannot swallow since my radiotherapy. Certain foods stick in throat and I feel choked. I also find apples bland and tasteless. As I could not, and would not throw away the apple which was given to me as prasad in the temple yesterday, I decided to try and eat it. After peeling it (to make it easier to swallow) after dinner, I was staggered—it was the juiciest, sweetest and most delicious God-given apple and I enjoyed it so much that I ate the whole thing without any problem with my swallowing. Thank You my God, it was so easy to eat coming directly from You.

14 June

On the way to work, I admired the dawn. The *surya* (sun) was just coming up, the blue sky had a smattering of pretty pink clouds. It was a little different today though, more breathtaking than other mornings. Normally I utter *Jai Surya Namaha*. I looked at the sun and the clouds whose hands were intertwined with each other to form a perfect 'Om'. Good God! At Redfern, an Indian lady passed by and gave me the sweetest smile. Lo! I saw Swami in that beautiful face!

Travel (24 June)

The urge, need, desire, call it what one may, had come upon me to go to Shirdi/Parthy. I asked the Baba's permission to give me a sign if They wanted me there. My favourite words 'Travel Travel Travel', have in the past been the Babas' sign to me to go. This morning, once I got on the train (that's where I had always seen the signs before – etched on train seats, windows, etc.), nothing similar happened. So I said, 'Okay Babas it doesn't have to be today, take Your time with the sign to travel'. I got to work, opened my e-mail and there it was written: 'Travel Travel Travel'. Now to arrange for the travel—that will be done. Thank You, the Babas, for such a quick reply.

27 June
I got the most amazing smell on the train of lilies from Minto to Leumeah stations, then looking at the sky, which was bright blue, I saw Shirdi Sai's (scarf and all) form as a massive white cloud, blessing me with His right hand. *Om Sai Shri Sai Jai Jai Sai.*

July

1 July
I went to the cashier for petty cash and was very happy to get the beautiful darshan of Swami from a picture of one of the ladies' desk in the Finance Department. Her name was Kamala. I got excited to see Swami 'out of the blue' so I asked her if she wanted some vibhuti. We talked about Swami. Oh such joy for us both!

Vibhuti (18 July)
I started the Saptaha of *Sai Satcharita*. I was in a hurry flurry to get to the article on *Travel*. In the excitement of getting it typed, I made a few errors. I will correct the same tomorrow. While it was an extremely busy and fulfilling day, I noticed many a times, during the day, the smell of vibhuti, which was sometimes very strong. I was very happy to have had this beautiful grace from the Babas at work. Even while I opened the *Sai Satcharita* on the train and in the office, the smell was there along with bursts of the smell of chandan. Thank You God for Your Grace.

Shirdi Temple (28 July)
I went to my Beloved's home at Strathfield for the first aarti. He very kindly and graciously let me be the first to do the aarti. I was at last comfortable with doing aarti. Joy, bliss! I left after aarti and received a lift to the station. I met Mum for lunch, went to the Indian place at 'Cockle Bay'. When ordering at the counter, the sweet young man

serving us made a comment to me, 'Madam, you look very pretty in your clothes' (I was wearing kurta). I said thanks and that I had been to the Temple. He asked, which temple. I told him the Shirdi temple in Strathfield. He and his friend looked aghast, they were both from Shirdi village and were here in Australia to work for a short period. What a Guru! He brings us all together in the strangest of places. I got so excited at meeting them, that I gave them a picture of Baba. Oh the joy on their faces at seeing their Baba!

August

Dream (5 August)

A dream about my beloved Shirdi Sai. I was in a hall, where Rita was also present and had asked me to help her to cook some food. I put too much water in the food. The room was filling up with people. I was running around looking for suitable clothes to wear, eventually sitting amongst a group of women. I was holding a picture of Shirdi Sai, a woman looking at it made a comment, I said, 'Yes, He is God, He is everywhere, sometimes if you look hard you may see Him. He is always watching us'. I saw Prasanna, a dear friend from our bhajan group, and her sons. We hugged each other. I started to cry. Harish, her son, told me that Prasanna was going away. We were then preparing for a bhajan. The dream ended. It was 5.15 a.m. (This dream sadly enough came true, our beloved Prasanna left her mortal coil on 25 July 2005 at the young age of 46). May her soul rest in peace.

12 August

I pray that this dream from Swami, comes to pass. There was a large dark room where people had gathered. There was a small room by its side. Swami was there, He called me to Him. I proceeded to manifest a very beautiful heavy gold lingam. Swami placed the same around my neck and said, 'I/this will always protect you'. I was ecstatic. I don't recall thanking Swami in my ecstasy, I do now though. I ran to the next room straight to Radha to show it to him. I turned around to see Swami giving Divine Darshan to all. My dream ended here. Thank You Swami, please make this dream come true.

17 August

Radha and Rita, friends from our bhajan group, visited me tonight. I love their sweetness. As usual, we chatted for a long time, and I asked them at one stage to take a look at Swami's Divine Feet in the puja room. The beautiful Lotus Feet had something inside the frame, which looked like a dried substance which had appeared all over Swami's Feet behind the glass. Being the simpleton that I am, I was not sure what this was and did not know who or what to ask about this. Therefore, when Radha and Rita came over, I hoped that they could enlighten me as to this beautiful sight, while at the same time, my heart longed for it to be a manifestation from Swami. I did not wish the ego to raise its ugly head. They looked at the picture and stated very definitely that it was a manifestation. I could only humbly state *koti koti pranaams* Swami, much love and thanks from me to Thee Swami. I had seen many pictures around Australia with the materialisation of udhi/vibhuti on them. This did not look like udhi/vibhuti but it was definite 'something'.

18 August

Fifteen people had come to bhajans. They were very simple and sweet. Tears overtook me completely especially at one stage when I looked at Swami's forehead and I could see a white 'Om' outlined quite clearly on it. Then to make it even clearer, I beheld a straight white light, akin to a torchlight, shining on the 'Om'. *Koti koti pranaams* my beloved Swami.

Wow! (22 August)

At japa today, I requested Swami to please give me one more affirmation that this was a manifestation (the picture of the Divine Lotus Feet in the puja room) of His and not a dream. A storm was on outside while I was doing japa. It was quite dark. Swami's face turned white, I felt Swami's presence staring at me from the picture. I was shocked but happy. Swami had immediately confirmed my question to Him. Thank You Swami. I wish I could live the rest of my life deserving God's Grace through His visions, dreams, vibhuti, and whatever else God wishes for me to have. I pray to be worthy of the same.

Shirdi Temple, Strathfield (25 August)

Abhishekam had started in Shirdi Temple. The pujari asked if I wanted to take part. He did not have to ask again. I washed Lord

Ganesh, Baba's Divine Lotus Feet, a lingam and murti which was quite heavy. Then I dried them, vacuumed the hall and helped the quiet lady (pujari's wife) who works tirelessly and silently. I did noon aarti, talked with Mr Tolani (the owner of the temple) and stayed for a delicious lunch. I felt very close to Baba, and decided to try to visit the temple when I could very happy and peaceful here. I was no longer feeling shy.

September

Darshan – A Sick Day (9 September)

I was very tired and not feeling too well. I left it to the Babas to give me a Sick Day if I was so deserving. At 5.45 a.m. I was lying on my right side facing the Babas on the wall. Shirdi Sai's face radiated darshan. I felt very peaceful; it was a very beautiful darshan and long too. Next I turned to Swami whose Divine Lotus Feet *lit up*. It was brief but beautiful; nothing can describe the Beauty of God's Light radiating from His Divine Body. Still debating whether to go to work, I sat up in bed, blew the nose and the tissue filled with blood. There was blood on the sheets too. I took this as a sign to have a 'day off'.

I had no choice but to stay home. After breakfast I received a beautiful darshan from Shirdi Sai's picture. Those eyes yet again! They pierce one's heart with kindness and love, one has to hold back from hugging the picture. Mere thanksgiving is never going to be enough. I can only give my heart and soul to You and offer You my pure love for You .

Ganesh Chaturthi (10 September)

Happy Birthday Lord Ganapati. He never drank the milk offered. I am sure Ganesh would have preferred laddoos. One day I would buy some for Lord Ganesha, but did Abhishekam in my simple way as I gave the remaining food to the birds They enjoyed it as there was nothing left on the plate. I love You Lord Ganapati, 'Gun Gun' as I call Him.

12 September

After dinner I spoke aloud to the Babas, 'I need some amrit for energy'. Radha arrived about 8 p.m. with honey. He had bought from a farm. I meant nectar from the Gods, but thank You, this was from You too.

A Miracle or Two (15 September)

At the Shirdi Temple, Strathfield, a lady gave us a picture. On the train I asked Baba why was there a line in the picture and I put it back in my bag. I got home, took the picture out but there were now two pictures. I immediately stated, 'I know I was given one picture, Shirdi Sai if You manifested this one, then there will be a picture of India in this magazine that I am reading and that will be Your affirmation that the second picture has come from You'. There were two pictures of India. *Koti koti pranaams* Muni. A devotee at the temple told us a lovely story about a few weeks ago. When they were about to clean Baba's murti before the temple closed, they removed the crown from His head and Baba's forehead was covered with udhi. God is and always will be on this earth.

20 September

On the way to work, I saw John (the guard on the train). I got darshan of Swami from John's carriage on the train. He loved Swami very much and his carriage was filled with Swami's pictures. He almost forgot to blow the whistle for the train to start, in his excitement of talking about Swami with me. Besides having a beautiful darshan of Swami, for which I was humbled and grateful, it was lovely to know such a devoted *bhakta* like John.

24 September

Today was a teary prayer session and intense indeed. Shirdi Sai's portrait was about to 'light up' but I had to rush off to work amid my tears. On the way to work, I just stepped outside the door. Swami looked His Best. The jet steam was against a perfect blue sky. It was so very beautiful. It felt like Swami was affirming 'See, I am with you'.

26 September

After an all night vigil, I could not sleep and the monkey mind never stopped. I was standing and watching the sky when I saw a beautiful jet steam. Good morning Swami.

A second later, there was another jet going by—good morning Shirdi Sai. I forgot the nightmarish night. I love and live for God's grace. They always put a smile on my face amid my gloom and tiredness. I was lucky a third time—there was another jet steam. The Babas were flying high, and so was I.

Happy Birthday My Beloved Everything, Shirdi Sai (28 September)

I didn't bake a cake but decided to cook from the Hari Krishna Recipe Book a *halwa* as prasad for Baba today, being His birthday. It looked very watery so I cooked it again and placed some at Baba's Divine Lotus Feet and the rest for prasad. But it still looked watery, so I cooked again for the third time, and then I returned it to the altar (I must confirm here that I am not a good cook especially Indian food, I am better at baking a cake or two). But before removing it once again I intoned to Baba, 'I hope You will at least have a wee bit of this food'. I then proceeded to take off the glad wrap and cooked it yet again. Some of it stuck on the plastic. It was the shape that astounded me, on closer inspection. There was a distinct BA with two little padukas' shape drawn. It was as clear as day. My sweet Lord had shown that He partook in my pathetic attempt at cooking *halwa*. I froze the rest, hoping it would get a little harder, the most important thing being He tasted and tested it. A cake next time Baba, more success with them.

30 September

Today I decided to bake cakes to sell for a good cause. I used the *halwa* on the top after coating it with chocolate icing. The cake was the first to sell and everybody loved it. The prasad was *halwa*. The *halwa* came to good use in the end.

October

Dream (1 October)

I had been literally begging the Babas to let me sleep, being awake from around 12.30 a.m. till 3.30 a.m. I eventually slept and I had a dream. In my dream I saw myself waiting for a fax to arrive. I ran to the machine when I heard it coming through. There were no words written, just a very large black and white picture of the most beautiful photo of Shirdi Sai, sitting very calmly (a hint to me perhaps, stay calm). This was followed by another page of a very happy Sathya Sai Baba (are You happy Swami that I am going to Prashanti?) When I awoke I could actually see Swami, in black and white with His blessing hand, very happy. I was very tired but very happy. Thank You the Babas. It was worth being awake. Was this a birthday blessing?

5 October

It being my birthday, I chatted with the Babas saying, 'You both get heaps of presents, attention, etc., I would like the same'. I was heaped with presents from my relatives and friends too. I don't know about the rest but I had a great time and the best was yet to come. Shirdi Sai's picture gave such real darshan. I cannot explain it. One has to witness such a miracle—His beautiful eyes and face.

What a Big Surprise—A Blissful Darshan (7 October)

I attended the prayers at 9.30 a.m. Before going for shopping with Mum, I asked Shirdi/Shiva, 'Is it okay for me to have a glass of wine to celebrate my birthday?' His eyes started to glow and I got a flash from the Shiva statue. Then I got to Shirdi Sai on the wall. I was stupefied. He was there looking at me, the light, the flesh, the eyes. My tears rolled, having never experienced such a blissful, full godly darshan. He was looking and listening so intently to me. You are awesome, blissful, beautiful Baba, no thanks is enough. Nothing can be compared to such Divinity as His.

Dream (12 October)

In my dream I saw myself seated in an open area, on a long table. It was evening, and opposite me sat Dad whose face was turned away as he was talking to a family friend, who was trying hard not to ignore me but gave me a wave. I waved back only to discover that my hands were covered in udhi/vibhuti. There was plenty of it too having an iridescence about it. There was so much of it on my hands that I tried to hide them under the table. My dream ended here.

The Day (15 October)

Eighty-four years ago on this very Tuesday, Shirdi Sai took Mahasamadhi. The Shirdi Temple celebrated this day from Saturday onwards. I took the day off today to go to the temple. He looked resplendent, brilliant, lustrous, and as beautiful as ever. The pujari and his wife did an excellent job yet again. I read a few pages of the *Sai Satcharita*, and was given the most pungent- tasting prasad rice. A very sweet lady dropped me to the station with Baba's Grace. I felt very lonely, I don't know why. During morning aarti, I did receive Baba's grace very beautifully indeed. All the pictures and statues in the puja room had the white light on each one of them, the candle on the altar at one stage became very dull and on looking at Shirdi Sai's picture, I saw him looking at me. I love Him, Swami and Jesus, and all, and know that He is ever alive and in most forms that I see.

November

Sweet Leela (10 November)

I was feeling very frail and tired. Looking at the altar at bhajans, after it was set up, I observed that once again there were no flowers put beside the picture of Jesus. I asked Swami to give Jesus a flower, as He had so many placed on His picture. I had barely finished my thought/sentence, than the flowers kept falling about —three of them, on Jesus' picture. Thank You Swami, I love You.

Leelas (18 November)

The jets were steaming across the sky. I felt blissful knowing that the Babas were flying high. I urged the Babas to let me be their typist. I barely sat at my desk, when I was called to the Report room short of clerical staff. So I typed till 4.00 p.m. and was ecstatic. You knew I loved to work, now didn't You think I deserve more pay? On the way home, I resisted plucking a gardenia, the most beautiful flower in the world to me, and even though we missed the first train, the second was delayed, and there was a beautiful fresh gardenia on the platform just waiting for me. I picked it up and took it home. I was spared from plucking the flower (I don't like doing this anyway, I feel like I hurt a flower when this is done). Baba placed it on the platform for me to pick up, no one else did.

Pain and Gain (19 November)

On opening the cupboard for cereal, I was shocked to see hundreds of black ants. I shut the cupboard and cried out for the Babas to remove them as I did not wish to slaughter any one of them. I went to work with a heavy heart.

At lunch while eating a sandwich, the two bottom front teeth fell out into my hand (Thank God I did not swallow them). I was horrified and embarrassed at the large ugly black hole staring out at me. I wished I was not so vai, and I am not. Hurriedly, I rang the dentist, who actually did fix it ($125.00), glued back two teeth in five minutes. Perhaps with my luck I wished I was a dentist, next life perhaps!

After work I opened the cupboard for a tea bag and not an ant was there in sight. The Babas heard me and had taken them away and given me back my teeth too. I love You and thank You the Babas.

23 November

A very Happy Birthday Swami. The cake baked was made with *pure love*. Please let it be blessed and be enjoyed by You. At noon aarti, I got a brief but very beautiful darshan from Swami's picture with the flower. I was a little taken aback by the suddenness of Swami's darshan and today of all days. I moved on to Shirdi Sai when Swami's darshan was over and asked Him if that really happened. Shirdi Sai's face lit up with the white Light confirming that it certainly did happen. Happy Birthday Swami, I love You and once again thank You.

December

God Bless Kala (6 December)

Kala took me to the hospital for an oesophageal dilatation and stayed with me from noon to eight o'clock in the evening. She was a very kind lady and a dedicated nurse. Before going into the theatre, I noticed my chart number was 36 (which adds up to number nine—the figure '9' is indicative of nine types of devotion described in chapter 21 of the *Sai Satcharita*). I was very happy and calm, while in the bay, a sister came by to check my details on the chart, looked at me and said, 'Be Happy'. While I awaited the results I thanked Shirdi Sai and Sathya Sai, Jesus and team, and Kala. I even had a dream when I came out of the theatre, where I saw Swami sitting very casually very close to me looking rather pensive and sombre. Swami said something but I don't know what it was. I awoke. I went to sleep only to see a statue of Shirdi Sai in the corner of a room looking at me. The Babas were with me and watching over me in the hospital. Thank You.

Darshan—My God (15 December)

I was a little worried at this time. I had the most awesome darshan at the altar room. The face of Shirdi Sai went berserk—a white cloud had covered His face completely. Shirdi on the wall was incredible. The cloud was thick and intense, and I could see the faces of my Gods one by one, first Swami then Shirdi, then Jesus then the Guardian angel. It was awesome, the wings were white and she looked like she was about to fly away. I felt scared, so undeserving of such Grace. I rang Rajshree (a good friend of mine, whom I call the wise one) who certainly knew the answers—all are one, God is in everyone; Christmas was round the corner and the Angel symbolised that. Thanks Rajshree for your wise explanation.

Darshan from Jesus and Our Lady (22 December)
I received beautiful darshan from the pictures of The Sacred Heart of Jesus, the Divine Mercy and also our Holy Mother, a beautiful assurance that they had heard my prayer and knew my sadness around the Christmas season. Thank You Jesus and Holy Mary for hearing my prayer and Your beautiful quick darshan. I love You.

Thank You Jesus (26 December)
It was a very merry Christmas indeed. Everybody was happy, we laughed, we ate, drank and had a very happy family Christmas. I thanked Jesus, Shirdi Sai, Sathya Sai, Mary and all. I prayed that all our Christmas's together be blessed by Them. I thanked Them also for the very beautiful and thoughtful gifts received. May I list some just for the memories:
From God—His grace and blessings and a peaceful and happy Christmas;
From Mum—$50, a scratch lottery, jam, wine, foot massage;
From Lisa—a book titled *Food of India* (a hint from the Babas I need to learn to cook Indian food), digital diary, soap, CD and her picture;
From the Lobos—$50 Sussan voucher, lemon soap;
From the Newells—a bottle of wine;
From Jeff, Merrilee and India (my niece and yes her name is India)—a gorgeous nightsuit ;
From my boss—$150;
From Kala and Henry—a beautiful blue silk salwar;
Thank You God and all the beings of the human kind.

Grace (27 December)
The gardener did the backyard and kindly took the gardenias home, while we were away in India (my Shirdi Sai and I).

The darshan received from Shirdi Sai and Sathya Sai and even a wee bit from Jesus, was awesome today. I would never be able to explain fully how very beautiful it was once again and it had been quite a long time too. I had no fear seeing God in His many forms, especially prior to a journey, it was His way of showing He loved me and was with me. I only wish it would never stop and I will continue to be greedy and ask for His Grace. For the rest of my life let His Will be done. Thank You God for 2002.

Puttaparthi (31 December)
It was good to be home again. I arrived in Parthy at 5.30 a.m. very tired and hungry, but could not settle till I had a shower. Then I walked to have Swami's at darshan 9.30 a.m., saw the crowds outside and I joined in. I was sure it was all over before I got there and I apologised to Swami for my lethargy and swooniness. Bhajans were going on and I saw the Lord. After aarti I first saw the beautiful Lotus Feet from behind gracefully walking towards His Divine Abode. What a sweet and memorable surprise to have this very beautiful darshan of Swami. Most grateful dear Swami. I also heard the voice of the Imam on my arrival (Shirdi Sai was showing that He was with me). I went onto the balcony, listened to the Imam and shed a tear. It was too beautiful. *Allah Ho Akbar Ho Allah.*

2003

January

A happy and peaceful New Year to the world.

Darshan (1 January)

The crowds were as big as the Kumbh Mela and the Seva Dals did their duty professionally, and all were seated. There were two queues instead of the normal one, right next to me in the other queue was Gaby. She did not recognise me. We had hugged and hoped we would meet again in Parthy. She looked very serene. I was on the verge of tears and I asked the Babas for laughter not tears and got the same on entering the hall. I put the pillows against one of the columns wondering why no one was sitting in this vacant spot, with a good view, only to realise a minute later why—'the pooing pigeons' were seated above the column. I chuckled to myself, as all of us humans tried to avoid pooed by the birds and kept looking up. But God was in good humour, the pigeons were above and there were no accidents, only we have been intolerant and anxious. I said to a girl sitting near me, that it was Swami's Will not ours, that compelled even the pigeons to obey Him and behave well. The darshan was very beautiful and I got an absolute clear view of Swami. I had not cried. The crowd at one stage got uncontrollable, I felt sorry for the Seva Dals. We all wanted to begin the New Year seeing Swami. At about 7.50 a.m. I asked Swami's permission to have breakfast. I laughed at my greed and need, as no breakfast was served on that day, due to all the chefs being at Swami's feet. I went back to the tree, sang the bhajans instead. The sweet boy at Sai Sadan gave me a sweet for the New Year. This was so kind of a poor boy who worked so hard and did not have much for himself. I prayed that may God fill this year with Grace for the family, friends and myself and may there be peace in the world. Swami cut a beautiful cake and photographs were taken amid cheers, I never received any prasad. I noticed Swami's aura today—it was white—exactly like the white aura I saw in the puja room at home.

I visited my Baba in the garden, the rose was still there. I sat on the stone in front and wished a Happy New Year. Then I broke three petals from the rose and with prayers stuck the first one on. After removing my finger I noticed it had taken the shape of an *Om*. Thank You Baba, *Sai Ram* Swami. I stuck the other two on and was so happy that my beloved Baba had heard my humble prayer as they stayed on.

Leela : While standing in the dinner queue I intoned Shirdi Sai, 'Time for some darshan from You to me'. My kameez was pulled by a girl who was very deformed. She was standing in the dinner queue behind me. I gave her some money and she in turn gave me a picture of Baba—I in You and You in me. Then I whispered into my chest, 'You choose whatever You like for dinner Baba, as we are sharing the same, but You choose, I will choose the dessert.' When we came to selecting a dessert I saw this delicious sweet, and I requested the lady at the counter for the same. She shook her head and said, 'No, you take this one tonight (a different sweet) and have that one tomorrow'. What could I say, He knew what dessert He preferred, and I did ask Him to choose, though I asked Him about the dinner not the dessert. Anyway His choice was delicious.

2 January

I had such a beautiful darshan from Swami today. I saw the Pink Twins, (these two beautiful ladies were from Brisbane, Australia; they visited Swami often and always dressed in pink, everybody at the Nilayam know them). What a delightful pair all dressed in pink yet again! I bought Connie Shaw's *Wake Up Laughing*. I saw a girl carrying the most beautiful purse with my Muni on it. I was waiting for Him to give me the same too. I had searched all the shops for this, but He did not want me to have the same.

Line 9 (3 January)

I made it for Suprabhatam. I just missed Omkar. I stepped out of the hotel to a cool, strong gust of wind, so refreshing, so peaceful like God was saying, 'Good morning Lorraine'. I walked in the bliss of this beautiful haven of peace. My Muni was shining above. I got the ninth line. This was God's number. I had beautiful darshan from

Swami. I started reading *Wake Up Laughing* and cried a lot on the first page.

Line 16—Sai Seva: Such Joy (4 January)

After darshan I hired a car. I bought twenty-five blankets. The poor boy (from Sai Sadan) carried them all for me. I was astounded that even though we were all in PN where I did all the shopping, no one came forward to give us a helping hand to carry the loads. I visited the boy's village, met his family, I loved the people, the goat, and my Muni was standing there watching me and even asking for a blanket. He got the last one, I took it off the driver for Muni. I distributed 100 kgs of rice. They were all so happy and laughed when we took photographs. I loved the simplicity and sweetness of the village people, their hearts were open, their eyes kind and they always had a smile on their faces.

Line 13 (5 January)

I had a good darshan of Swami. Anil Kumar as usual, was extremely interesting his topic being 'Dreams and Visions'. I was happy to see Mrs Kottieth and Radha who were here for a day. We went to Swami'`s birthplace, to a beautiful temple complex where there was a small temple of Shirdi Sai too. I was very happy that Radha got up close and I had a personal darshan from Swami and also His prasad, a fig, which he shared with us. I was very grateful for this as it was from Swami directly.

The Ghost (7 January)

I had morning tea at Gaby's (we did finally meet again and she invited me to tea) beautiful apartment in Parthy. It was well-furnished and well lit. Over a delicious cup of Sage Tea we were discussing Diane's (my best friend in Cairns,) illness. I commented that I felt it was a 'possession' due to the spirits/ghosts that literally filled her home in Australia. Gaby agreed with me as she had seen a possessed woman in her room next door at Parthy, a few years ago. While talking, we both noticed a figure go past the window. It looked like Swami going by. Gaby looked aghast as there were no balconies near the window or even across the house over the road. I ran out to affirm this. There was no balcony. It was like seeing a ghost walking in air. We sat down to tea and the head passed by again. Our mouths dropped. To me it came over as a confirmation from Swami that Diane was possessed. *Sai Ram*. On the way home after dinner I noticed a car bedecked with flowers and four lads sitting near it. It also had a light shining on the photos of Shirdi Sai, Swami and Hanuman. I was curious and asked one of the lads what this was about. They stated that they had walked from Mumbai to Parthy and were waiting for accommodation. God Bless them; it made me cry—mere lads and such devotion! I thanked the Lord for such a day. After returning to Australia, I spoke to Diane about the incident. She had never contacted me again.

Line 15 (9 January)
I went to the puja room at Sai Sadan. On the altar was a frame with the Lotus Feet of Swami filled with vibhuti and *akshata*. I helped myself to the akshata. It was an experience of the Godly kind. They did love me. On going back to the room, the adopted son (the boy who looks after me in the hotel) gave me a beautiful statue of my beloved Shirdi Sai.

Line 10 (10 January)
I received good darshan from Swami in the Sai Kulwant Hall, and even though I was in line ten, I could see Swami very clearly. Thank You Swami. Five more days went by and I had still not made to line one (or was there no interview from Swami?). I met an interesting Italian lady. We had similar thoughts on the dinner-line crashers and a good laugh together too. (For meals in the canteens here, one had to stand in line. Some of us stood in the queue early while some came in just before the doors to the canteens opened and walked straight in, without standing in queue. It was annoying as we did the right thing and stood in line, like all were supposed to do). The dinner/lunch crashers, did crashed their way in and were therefore fed first, while the rest waited in the queue. We even complained at Swami's lodge. Humans after all. The boy at Sai Sadan bought me some keyrings with the Babas on it and a silver bracelet with '*Om Sai Ram*' on it. God bless him and his family, so poor and yet so kind and generous and thoughtful!

Sports Day (11 January)
Everything was closed for the sports meet. I had a lovely sleep last night with my Shirdi Sai beside me (He had a fall earlier in the day when the boys were cleaning and dusting the room they

accidentally dropped Baba's statue. So I had rubbed some Tiger Balm on Him and hopefully He was not too sore). I met a very interesting looking man in the garden; he was very skinny, tall and with striking eyes. Of course I was immediately reminded of Him. The man was trying to lift the rock with Zorasthra (a spiritual figure worshipped by the Persians) on it. I advised him to be careful as it was embedded in the mud and was very heavy. He asked me where I was from, and said I didn't look like an Indian. I said I felt very Indian and then bade him farewell. It was just behind Shirdi Sai's stone. Sometimes I feel so strongly that it is Him who comes in human form to talk with me.

Line 8 (12 January)

Being a Sunday there were many people. I was very happy to get a great view of Swami. Swami stopped outside before entering. We were like facing each other for a minute. I received no glance from Swami but His Divine standstill darshan was good enough for me. In my dream last night, I was talking of Jesus in India and about Swami. Leslie, a friend, said something in Sanskrit. It was very impressive. Sharon, my sister, was looking nonplussed while I fumbled with my 'talk'. I noticed a movie on a wall, Swami was in it pointing to a wall. The wall collapsed, then Swami pointed His finger and the wall went back again. I was distressed, everyone seemed to be showing Swami a different light. My dream ended here.

Line 5—Shankranti Day (13 January)

I was at my usual spot, and had beautiful darshan. I enjoyed Sarah Pavan's talk reminding us that God is the Doer. We have to remember that. I was up for most of the night as the loudspeakers blared till 5 a.m. I prayed for saburi and acceptance. I was feeling sad on having to leave in a few days. I could not sleep and went onto the balcony at 2 a.m. to view a beautiful black sky with the stars merrily twinkling and a jet steam going by at this hour. Swami was not asleep either. I had darshan of Shirdi Sai twice in picture/human form. He gave me vibhuti and blessings. Thank You Baba.

14 January

I went to Chaitanya Jyoti. I saw my Shirdi Sai on the way (the new statue in the sports ground). I wished they could place an umbrella over Him, as usual He was exposed to all the elements, and then had to stand all day and night poor Baba. While Chaitanya Jyoti was a very lovely museum there was not too much mentioned about Shirdi Sai which disappointed me. It was very modern and technological. I did like the film of Swami in Badrinath wearing a hat, riding a donkey and wearing sunglasses. It was very humbling and very human.

Line 15 (15 January)

Since Swami did not take the letters given to me by devotees in Australia, they were posted. I thanked Swami, and was now off to Bangalore. I stopped at the Shirdi Temple on the way back, in time for a lovely puja/Homam. It was the day of Pongal, a very auspicious feast in South India. I threw some wood into the dhuni twice along with the nine grains. I meditated, got some lovely prasad then arrived at St. Marks hotel in Bangalore at 2.00 p.m., safe and sound. I had always wanted my palms to be read in India, a method called Nadi. Therefore, I sought through the telephone directory to find a good astrologer, if this is what they are called. The first page I opened in the telephone directory read NADI, but it costed Rs 1500 and there would be no tape recording of the session held. I could not sleep and was up with a headache. I fell off to sleep eventually but was suddenly woken up at 5.15 a.m. with a soft beautiful female voice saying 'Hello' in my ear. On waking up there was no one there, just the voice!

Be Aware (16 January)

After visiting Thayeammas, the children, and the Shirdi Temple in Ulsoor, Baba looked sweet and calm but no flowers were given to me this time and no ghostly appearance from Him. I went to the place recommended in Bangalore to view the vibhuti materialisation. A man (big) in a loin cloth greeted me at the door and told me to leave my bag on a chair and to relax. I was uncomfortable from the start. There was a little shrine where his sister was praying, saying she would bless me when she finished. I could see no materialisations on the pictures and started to feel more uncomfortable. The man said to me, 'Don't be so nervous'. He then went to the front room where my bag was and pulled the curtain. I felt uneasy at this so I got up and went to the room where he was, only to find he had opened my bag and was just about to take the money out of it. I had Rs 30,000 in the bag, most of it belonging to Kala in Australia who wanted me to buy her a gold chain from India. I grabbed the bag from him and told him he should be ashamed of himself, posing as a pujari. Then I ran down to my car shaking in shock and told my driver what had happened. I was saved by the Babas. Here was a thief in the guise of a priest putting fake ash on pictures and luring people into his home and all in the name of God, robbing innocent tourists.

17–18 January

I had Bhrigu/Nadi done. Before the session, I surrendered to Shirdi Sai to let His Will be done and speak to me through the man doing the reading. I found the reading extremely interesting as the first thing the man said to me was Your Ishta Devata is Shirdi Sai and you are also very fond of Ganesha. How right he was! I left for Mumbai got to Dharmakshetra at 6.00 a.m. and was gruelled by the caretaker of this place, who scratched his back and front so profusely that I was sure he had a nest of nits in both areas. We argued and phoned for a car. He did give me his tea though at about 9.30 a.m. By this time I was parched. I gulped it down realising where his fingers had been and almost vomited. At long last, after he was so sure I would *not* get on a bus, he relented and we hired a car to drive me to Shirdi. He took me to the bank in his car. I had to pay his driver Rs100, just to take me to the bank, two minutes away (what happened to seva?), while he baulked at the poor driver. I paid Rs 3200 for the car to Shirdi. It looked big and safe and eventually, I left for Shirdi with two drivers (more hoodlums than drivers) hired for me. It was a horror ride to Shirdi. The drivers especially the owner an arrogant punk, turned up the Bollywood tunes on CD very loudly all the way. He seemed to be on a high. He was boorish, laughed and sang aloud and drove like a maniac. I shouted to slow down at one stage, but he just laughed. They took an hour's lunch break while I sat fuming in the car. After a few close shaves, I arrived at my Beloved's Abode at 4 p.m. It was a very long day indeed but I was so happy to be there. I was keen to have my first piece of food in fourteen hours. It was so good to see His portrait like the one at home in my bedroom. He was always looking at me and I prayed that He would never take His beautiful eyes off Lisa and me.

Shirdi (19 January)

I saw the most beautiful sunrise. It was spectacular and indescribable. There was God in His glory and Swami too in the jet steam going by. The day was already filled with God's Grace. I had cornflakes for breakfast; I did feel being pampered by Him. Vinnie, the author of *Ambrosia in Shirdi,* rang, and confirmed that we would be meeting the next day. My throat and nose were in a mess. Around 4 p.m. after having slept for most of the day, though the throat was very sore, I felt almost normal again. While sitting at the bay window, I was looking across to the most beautiful green paddy fields ahead. There was a thatched hut in the middle of it, with a simple and happy farmer family going about their chores. The boys just flew a kite quite high. The sun was beaming. The world was so serene, the swallows were flying around and I was with my Shirdi Sai in Shirdi. Vinnie and Sardhan visited around 6.30 p.m. They too loved Shirdi Sai. She gave me her new book and a yellow scarf touched to Baba's murti. I was glad it was not washed. I felt closer to Him. Thank you Vinnie and Baba.

20 January

I had a walk with Vinnie to all the places Baba used to walk through and I was sure that He still did. I went to the museum where my favourite picture of Him was. I received two roses and blessings from Abdul Baba's tomb and room. It was very distressing to have been told by people in Shirdi of the removal of Dixit's wada which was built when Shirdi Sai was there in mortal form. The branches of the peepul and neem trees had been cut and so much of desecration been done to the shrine. If Baba permitted, I liked to be an instrument along with Vinnie and Sardhan to stop this carnage and also to clean up the Samadhi and other areas. They treated it like a cesspool and the surrounding area certainly smelled like it. He was spoiling me rotten indeed. I bought a Shirdi kurta (as my Baba's gift to me) which I planned to wear the next day. I received pieces of chandan from Dwarakamai, vibhuti and stones from the dhuni, stones from the chavadi all crushed and poured into a small silver piece of jewellery which I wore on my neck, which Sardhan sealed for me the next day. My life was my Baba and my Baba was my life.

21 January

I woke up to hear the first aarti. It was very moving. I went to Sakori. It was lovely to see the Ganesh on the tree and I was blessed. Then I went to Korhala (Sardhan's temple) which was very sweet and beautiful. I was happy to see my Muni even having a *chhatra* over Him. The fields were covered with crops and were lush even though there was a drought. Shirdi Sai had taken care of it all. I bought eighteen glass bangles in Rahata. Baba used to go there to the Idgar Wall. We saw it, I touched it and cried, I felt like Shirdi Sai was resting up against it. I saw bale fruit and a beautiful tamarind tree. I shed a tear. I was reminded of my childhood. I felt very much like Shirdi Sai was with me, walking with me and showing me all the places He used to and still visit.

22 January

I had a chat with Baba (we had many chitchats together, He listened, I talked endlessly). I don't own Shirdi Sai. He belongs to the world, but I prayed that He owned me and took over my life completely. Sardhan took me to the Samadhi Mandir. I did not have to stand in the queue like the rest. I laid the *Sai Satcharita* on the Samadhi and also at the padukas. I was then called to the other side where the pujari took the *Sai Satcharita* from me, touched it to the Samadhi and Baba's feet at the murti and handed it back to me with a coconut and a bunch of roses, and the two security ladies were so sweet, they made room for me to do my pranaams. Thank You my most Beloved. Then I went to Dwarakamai where the words 'This Masjidmai will look after you' kept ringing in my ears. I bought a huge rose garland. The pujari in Dwarakamai beckoned me to Him, while he opened Baba's large wooden framed photograph for me to put the garland inside it. The garland broke at one end. It was like Shirdi Sai was helping us to hang the garland on Him. We installed the garland on Baba's picture, the pujari nailed it back. One lady made a protest she wanted to do the same. I had done *tirth* (pilgrimage), touched the padukas and asked for a safe journey. I touched the grinding stone and the lamps, and the washing stone and even got a chance to feed the beggars. Thank You my Beloved God for Your love and Grace and Sardhan/Vinnie too for all Your help.

23 January

Vinnie, Sardhan and I went to the auction in Shirdi. There was a gold embroidered shela which we bid for and won, but someone else took it. It wasn't meant for me I guess. Eventually I got three pieces. I was very sorry to leave Shirdi. I prayed for God's grace to send me to Parthy and Shirdi soon again. After paying the bill at the 'Sun-n-Sand' the manager's wife came to me and made a presentation at the front desk, as I had been staying at 'Sun-&-Sand' so many times. I was embarrassed and very surprised. I thanked all the staff who came out to bid me a fond farewell, especially the sweet door/porter man—we all knew each other so well by then. The gift was the most beautiful statue of Shirdi Sai. He did spoil me.

I arrived at Mumbai airport at 12 midnight not taking off till 5.30 a.m. the next day. A man stopped me and asked if I needed help. I told him I was very early. Nevertheless he escorted me to the Air India checkout counter which was closed. He took my ticket, and I opened my passport wallet to remove the same. He then placed his hand on the picture of my Shirdi Sai that I had in it and said to me, 'He is my God, surrender everything to Him and He will help you'. I said, 'He is my Everything and I have surrendered to Him.' He then gave me the best seat on the plane and told me his name was Prasad and left. What more can I say—Shirdi Sai was again there in human form!

February

11 February

I came home after a hot and hard day to find that the picture of Swami in the bedroom had fallen face down and the glass was completely shattered. I was extremely upset not for the glass having broken but for poor Swami lying on His face surrounded by glass. 'Talking too much', perhaps this was the message. I really don't like being in many places, what can I do though. I have a problem with speaking my mind, but I seek and speak the truth.

23 February

The story below written by me had been published earlier in *Sai News Australia* (Special 77th birthday issue, p. 33) titled 'Prince of Clowns'. My humble thanks to Swami. We did have a sense of humour and laughter, after all, love was the best medicine. The story went as:

There is a little statue of Lord Ganesha in the kitchen at home and behind it is a calendar of Baba. One Sunday, I went to clean that area, (to be precise, Baba and Ganesha are sitting on the microwave), on looking at both the picture and statue, my heart started to beat rapidly, as there appeared to be a white powder on the picture as well as the statue. Golly, at last, God has seen fit to grace me with some vibhuti. I was too excited to do anything but stand and stare at this 'phenomenon' for a while. The next stage (so goeth the monkey mind), would be to ring one of the other Sai devotees to ask them to come over to confirm this 'miracle'. The hours went by, but I somehow did not ring anyone. The day was spent looking at the picture and the statue and the white powder in bliss. Could not sleep at night, my heart so desired this to be vibhuti, and my mind thought of nothing else, but reality and recollection struck the next morning as to what the white powder really was, and how I laughed and cried at the same time.

A few weeks ago I was given a box of Turkish Delight, covered with white sugar always sharing my 'spoils' with the Babas. I remember putting a piece of this on Baba's mouth before me eating the same. Alas, not vibhuti but Turkish Delight. I can assure you reader, I was not delighted.

Dancing with Rainbows (28 February)

I made a vow to Lord Shiva to repeat *Om Namah Shivaya* 9,000 times leading up to Shivaratri on 1 March 2003.

Before leaving for work, I touched Shiva's statue and said, 'Have I reached, exceeded or got near the 9000 *Namah Shivayas* yet?' I opened the front door to see the most beautiful rainbow just above the house; it then doubled. On walking further there were two more rainbows. I beamed; it was Shiva's sign to indicate that I had reached my 9000th *Namah Shivayas*. On nearing the station I noticed that there was not a big rainbow or part of a rainbow but little rainbows scattered everywhere. I got into a state of euphoria. I felt like reaching out to them and dancing under the rainbows and in their colours. At the station I got a bit greedy and said in and to my heart, 'if this is truly what I saw and not imagined, let me see three more rainbows before I board the train'. There they were another three rainbows. I don't know if anyone else noticed this Divine leela. *Om Namah Shivaya*.

March

Mahashivaratri—Om Sign (1 March)

I rushed back home after shopping at the mall, trying to do everything and then have a bit of rest. I was standing at the kitchen window, cloud watching (clouds always make me feel relaxed). A cloud stopped still, it was a perfect 'Om'. Shiva's night was beautiful as usual, the bhajans were excellent and I loved the bael leaf offering ceremony. These rituals were new to me and I did so enjoy them even if I didn't understand them. I felt very close to the Babas. Shiva's statue was resplendent with tiger skin and I experienced a very beautiful night.

Jesus and the Red Gerbera (Flower) (12 March)

I went to church at lunchtime where I worked. I loved the statue of Jesus on the Cross, it always moved me. I went in, sat down and noticed a very beautiful red gerbera flower placed between the Holy Feet of Jesus. It was stuck right in between the Feet. It looked so pretty and fresh and my eyes kept going towards it. I whispered to Jesus requesting Him to give me the same. I continued my prayers, lit some candles and went to pray at The Holy Feet. Just as I got to the statue, the red gerbera fell at my feet. Thank You Jesus, I love You and You made a sad lady very happy with Your Divine leela, (Jesus knows what a leela is, He gives many).

Seeing God in Little Things (18 March)

I went outside at about 6.30 a.m. to observe the full moon but could not see it. Instead I saw the beautiful morning star shining brightly. It was like looking at Shirdi Sai sitting and swinging from it. It was very bright and beautiful. The sky was gorgeous as were all the other twinkling stars. I was looking directly at God's work.

While travelling to work, in the train, I was reading *Sanathana Sarathi*, a piece from Swami about seva. I had asked Swami to clarify what is meant by seva, is it extra work to be done in addition to our normal duties? There was an article published in *Sanathana Sarathi* about seva. Swami answered my question. This was further confirmed when I got the most powerful aroma of roses, strong, overpowering and beautiful. None had roses on the train.

I was walking through Newtown. The sky had turned a magnificent blue. There was a rosella (bird-parrot in India) nearby.

I could almost touch it. Thank You God for allowing me to see and smell Thee in nature, in the beauty of Your work.

19 March

I went outside on waking up as I could see that the moonlight had brightened the backyard and it was like looking at God once again through the beauty of the full moon. It was a pity that I saw God in nature and not so much in mankind.

I saw God again on my way to work. The sky was an azure blue and there was Swami symbolised in the jet steam. Against the blue sky and the sun, Swami looked gorgeous and at one point as the jet was flying high but slowly, there was a cloud shaped like an 'Om'. Maybe my imagination do run away with me sometimes, but the truth was what I saw and felt. On nearing the Redfern station, I looked out of the window and saw God jetting by again. I had two darshans in one day. *Sai Ram.*

The Dentist (25 March)

When I visited the dentist, as usual, I was in a nervous stupor. The anaesthetist was introduced to me by the dentist. Those eyes looked so familiar. He asked me where I was from (the anaesthetist not the dentist). I said India, he said he was also from India, South India, and that his name was Dr Pai (I heard right Pai not Sai). He then proceeded to put the needle into my hand, he being so gentle. When I awoke, he was sitting by my side. He gave me an orange juice and when I was able to walk, he led me to a comfortable chair in another room. I then knew, from the eyes that in the guise of Dr Pai, He was my Shirdi Sai and Swami, the dentist.

April

Darshan (7 April)

I started reading *Sai Satcharita* for Ram Navami. As it is stated in the *Sai Satcharita* 'this work should be read at home specially on Guru-Poornima, Gokul-Ashtami, Rama-Navami and Dasara [Baba's Anniversary day]' (epilogue), I try to read the *Satcharita* during these festivals. I felt Swami was on His way to Sai Kulwant Hall. He flashed past there while I was praying. It was good to see the Light shining from Swami's beautiful face. It was a short but sweet darshan.

15 April

I went to church in search of palms (it was Palm Sunday). I went past the table at the entrance. There were no palms. I chanted the prayers, broke two strips from the fronds at the altar (with the permission of Jesus) on the way out, and to my surprise, noticed a palm lying on the same table. There was none there earlier on the way in. Thank You Jesus.

The Lord Has Come D-Day (Dentist) (22 April)

I was extremely nervous to undergo more surgery on my teeth. I begged the Babas to be with me. At aarti just before finishing, I asked Shirdi on the wall to look after me. (Please let me take the opportunity to explain that I have to frequently visit a dentist due to my having cancer of the nasopharynx in the past, treated by surgery and radiotherapy. I fully recovered but have been left with a mouthful of ailing failing teeth and gum problems due to the radiation to that area, and also not having any saliva. It has now come to the stage when my mouth area is so sensitive that I have to be anaesthetised in order for a dentist to continue with the teeth). Before going to the dentist, I received the most beautiful and awesome darshan. Baba's kafni glittered and He was so real, I felt like He was saying, 'See, I am with you, don't be afraid'. I received a double blessing, when a rippling light beam fell on the big pink picture of Shirdi I was looking at . I could not believe my eyes. The reality was such that the only thing that never occurred was to hear Baba speak, as He was certainly there in body and spirit. *Koti koti pranaams*, my humble thanks will never be adequate.

May

Darshan at the Bookstore (16 May)

I visited Adyar bookshop in Sydney City after a long time. It had been renovated with a lot more space and a beautiful statue of Ganesh at the entrance. That made my heart flutter. Indulged by the Babas, I bought two books, one I was positive I had read before *Daughter of Fire* by Irene Tweedie who found a Sufi master when she was in her fifties in India and became a Sufi herself. Second was *The Sai Prophesy* which I could not go past.

18 May

I awoke and the first idea that came to my mind was that wouldn't it be just right if by God's Grace, we could open up our own bookshop? I got so excited that I left this beautiful idea to Him. Strangely enough, during the course of the day, I received an invitation from Lisa asking me to attend The Book Show with her next Saturday. A Divine sign? I had to let God do what He wills. Maybe a book or shop would come later in my life (a dream I had always had especially having a book shop). We attended the show and it was good, especially one of the lectures given by an Indian author, whose name I am not able to recall. I ended up buying *White Mughals* by William Dalrymple.

Dream (20 May)

I dreamt of Swami. It was another restless night. I spent most of it reading *The Sai Prophesy*, and finally fell off to slumber to have but a dream of Swami. I saw Swami wearing a white robe, and me sitting beside Him on the floor and we were covering books. Swami said to me, 'We will sell these for $2 each.' Then a host of friends and relatives entered the room, who were very loud and unruly. Swami went away and I watched in despair at their behaviour, but could not state that this was a very sacred place and Swami was there. Then I tried to get some food but manoeuvering through some hot heavy steamy pots. I don't remember the end of the dream but on waking up I saw an orange glow near the bedroom door which looked patterned. I felt like Swami had just walked through there. I closed my eyes and fell off to sleep again. I was very humbled and happy that Swami allowed me His Divine darshan through a very longed for dream. I looked at the mail box *before* going to work to find *Sanathana Sarathi* there. Swami certainly had been present.

June

Kala's Story (6 June)

What a lovely story Kala had today! At last she was seeing the signs and experiencing the bliss. She was meditating on the Gayatri picture. The picture started to glow and she saw a thin film of vibhuti on Swami's hand. She touched it and the vibhuti came onto her finger. I was very happy for Kala. She was certainly deserving of

God's Grace. I prayed that she and Henry may have further beautiful experiences.

9 June
I went to my Shirdi Temple at Strathfield in time for the Shej aarti. My Baba was resplendent in pink and I was very happy to see familiar faces although I was more comfortable with books rather than people. Baba graciously allowed me to do aarti. I received *halwa* as prasad and even handed the bell while Mr Tolani, owner of the temple, did his aarti. I was grateful for the seva. After aarti, I went to bid farewell to Dr Vithi, who was also at the temple, who in turn looked at the pujari and said, 'She bakes very nice cakes'. I was happy and surprised. I don't know how Dr Vithi remembered this as it was very rarely that I met him. I had started working on the diaries again. When I started typing I got a very strong smell of camphor. Perhaps one day I might be the instrument/author of a Sai book, if Baba was willing.

Swami's Darshan (11 June)
At the Central Station, before getting off, there was an Indian lady talking to her husband. The train was just about to stop. I noted that she was wearing a ring with the image of Swami on it. I was so happy seeing Swami in this form and in such a place as busy as the Central Station. I touched the ring spontaneously and said *Sai Ram* to her and she replied *Sai Ram* and smiled. Thank You very much Swami for Your very sweet darshan. It was certainly appreciated, please stay close to me.

21 June
I went to Liverpool to shop for some reason but did not walk along the normal route. I took a detour. I noticed a sign inside an arcade 'Sai Gold'. Of course, Swami led me to the shop and I was ever so happy to see Swami's picture inside the jeweller's shop. Then also at the 'Taras' where I went for Indian groceries, I saw all the Gods were on display giving darshan except my Shirdi Sai. My heart was heavy at not seeing Him. I finally found Him hiding, sitting humbly, all in silver, and my heart jumped for joy.

22 June
The bhajan session was held at Banu and Srinis' (couple from our bhajan group) home. It was beautiful. The Babas were there, the

food was delicious. I had to have brunch in the puja room with the Babas, it felt like being in Shirdi/Parthy. I was very happy to see such a beautiful display of Ganesha and my God Shirdi Sai's, statues everywhere. Banu's parents had told me to go to Thane near Shirdi where there was a beautiful temple of Shirdi Sai. I noticed an advertisement in the Indian papers yesterday. Should I consider this as my signal to book a ticket to Shirdi/Parthy?

July

The Journey Ahead—Darshan (6 June)

It was safe to arrange the trip to India—Shirdi, Goa, and maybe, Mysore. The word 'Travel' had appeared in the papers along with a few other words to go, from the Babas, but still I was hesitant and unsure. I asked for darshan as the final sign to write a book. On doing japa, darshan was awesome. The black/white picture of Shirdi Sai became white, His face becoming so real, I had to hold my breath, Swami too looked like He had a white veil covering His face. This was quite a unique scenario besides being beautiful. I decided to book the tickets for the trip.

Dream (11 July)

I was awake from 12.30 a.m. to 3 a.m. While doing the *Om Sai Ram pranaam* I wondered if I had reached the 9000th chanting in time for Guru Poornima. I asked the Babas to let me know if I had, and then I fell off to sleep to have a lovely but strange dream.

I saw that a few people had gathered, and saw Swami walk past in a white/silver robe. There were two men walking with Swami. I watched intently. Swami opened a door, leaned forward, extended His hand in a shake and whispered very softly good night. I realised it was my Nana Gladys that Swami was addressing. I was joyous. There were fireworks everywhere. Swami said, 'Go take, plenty for all'. I saw Rohit run to collect them. When he returned, he had three long large boxes of sparklers, which were very big. Rohit smiled at me and said he would give me one. I saw a few pictures lying around and there He was, my beloved Shirdi Sai, a small picture with His hand in blessing. I smiled, wept and stated, 'I knew You would be here' as I do so often to Him while awake. My dream ended.

Shirdi's Game (29 July)

I did not want to go to work today as I had another interview to go for a job (closer to home). Shirdi had a wonderful sense of humour and always came to my rescue, at the right time, without even having to ask. I woke up feeling really sick with a blocked nose, sore back, headache. I thanked the Babas for allowing me to be sick as it was too cold to go to travel for two hours to work and I had no excuse for staying home. I just wanted to stay in bed for half the morning and then go for an interview. I loved this leela. I got the courage to ring work to say I was not going in. Thank You God for being in cohorts with me. I never got the job though, so you see reader, He kept my wishes only halfway but He did give me a day off without my getting into trouble.

August

The Dentist (1 August)

I arrived at the dentist's clinic at 3 p.m. Dr Pai (no not Sai) started to put the needle in my hand and asked me, 'You are a Shirdi devotee, you are wearing His ring'. I nodded, he then said that he was a Shirdi devotee too. He then stated, 'Do you know of Sathya Sai and are you a devotee? I have heard about Him but don't know too much'. I fell asleep then. I felt the Babas were with me as just before entering the dentist I saw two jet steams above. Everything went well at the dentist and I felt no pain.

The Letterbox and Angel Card (2 August)

I decided to put some white vaseline on the keys hoping it would help to lock and unlock the letter box, which kept jamming. I did the aarti first and had a very beautiful darshan from the pink Shirdi photo, which made me weep. I asked Baba to help me with the broken letterbox. The letterbox was repaired and put back to order and the key could be inserted and opened with ease. I also received a call from the dentist, that I would not have to visit him for six months. *Sai Ram.*

Sai Leelas (4 August)

Sanathana Sarathi was in the letter box; it was not stolen as some other mail had been, due to the letter box being broken.

I could not sleep, staring at the ceiling wishing I would see the Angels. Here they were. The white cloud above Shirdi Sai's portrait in the bedroom hovered for a bit then disappeared.

Lisa had two wisdom teeth taken out without anaesthesia. She had little pain but she was okay. *Sai Ram*. She proved to be braver than her mother.

12 August

It was around 5.30 a.m. I was standing at the kitchen window eating breakfast. Shirdi Sai, in the form of the beautiful Morning Star was there staring at me from the sky in all His splendiferous glory. He was ever in my heart. I didn't need to see Him. He was just there and His presence was always felt by me, even though He did not show Himself in the flesh. I had pictures and statues of Shirdi Sai everywhere in the house, I never felt alone, and whatever I did or said, I tried to remember to include Him in it.

21 August

My knees were playing up badly while walking up the stairs at Leumeah station. I was praying that the driver on the platform would not blow the whistle loudly, as my ears were so sensitive. The train took off, about 200 yards on, the whistle was blown in the softest tone. I could not believe my ears. He answered my simple prayer in the quickest and kindest possible way. He knew how sensitive I was to sound.

26 August

With God's permission I have decided to name this home *Majida* (word taken from the book *Unravelling the Enigma* by Marianne Warren, and means *Masjid*). This was the name given to Shirdi Sai when He was a young lad.

The Dream (29 August)

In my dream I saw Swami coming out from behind a door, smiling, doing Abhaya Hasta. I watched while Swami bent forward His face observing the ground, while I observed Swami's beautiful, thick glossy hair with streaks of grey. He then stood erect and smiled. Someone handed me two packages. I gave one to Sharon my sister and looked at mine, feeling very pleased to see a picture of Hanuman on it and at His feet there was a little blue box containing some liquid. Someone asked what it was, I stated amrit. End of dream—I pray it would come true.

30 August

I went to the 'Tara's' to get some laddoos for Ganesh Chaturthi which was to be celebrated the following day. Ganesh loves them, but before leaving I had the most beautiful, awesome unexpected darshan from my beloved Shirdi Sai's pink picture. His eyes came to life, they moved, they glowed and they looked ever so kind and loving. How can one describe this phenomena in words—to see and know that God was looking at me with such love. I could not get humbled enough. He knew what was in my heart, words need not be uttered. I love You very much Sai.

A Sufi poem to my Shirdi Sai:

Oh love, oh pure deep love
Be here, now
Be all, worlds dissolved into your stainless endless radiance
Frail living leaving burn with you brighter than cold stars
Make me your servant, your breath, your core.

— Jelauddin Rumi

September

Om Shri Ganeshaya Namaha (1 September)

On the way to work, I asked Lord Ganesha, 'Did I repeat *Om Shri Ganeshaya Namaha* 1800 times on Saturday/Sunday? Please give me a sign'. I was about to cross the road, when a car beeped. I looked at the number plate and the number was 1806. It is 8.45 p.m. While writing this I am getting the fragrant smell of vibhuti. *Om Shri Ganeshaya Namaha.*

18 September

There was awful weather on the way home. I got off at Leumeah which was still dark and very windy with few but heavy drops of rain. I was praying to Shirdi to stop the gale and wind so we could get home safely. I looked up to see the most beautiful complete huge rainbow overhead. The weather changed in a second, the black clouds disappeared, the wind stopped, the sun came out and we got home safely. He had stopped the gale and had got me home safely.

Leelas (30 September)

On waking up I had prayed to experience God. I checked for e-mails at 5 a.m. as I could not sleep. I received the darshan of the Baba as someone had e-mailed me pictures of Baba.

At the Central Station, I saw the boy who looked just like a young Swami on another platform.

I rang the Shirdi Temple, and Mrs Banu said she would keep it open till I arrived.

The candle had burned form 6.30 a.m. to 6.30 p.m. twelve hours instead of nine. *Jai Sai Ram.*

One only needs to ask and he/she shall receive.

October

Travel Travel Travel (1 October)

A familiar word and what a lovely leela to start the month with. Whenever I see these words it has always been a confirmation from the Babas that I may proceed to Shirdi, Parthy or whichever place of Divinity they would like me to visit. Even though the travel plans were put into action since June, I was still uncomfortable that I had not yet seen those three important words. I whispered to Swami this morning, 'I don't feel too sure that You want me to be at Your Lotus Feet as I have not yet got the sign to travel. I hope You will oblige today (a birthday present from You to me)'. Around 3 p.m. a fax came through at work for one of the doctors. I picked up the same to take it to his office. It was from his travel agent. I could not stop smiling and thanking Swami, the word 'Travel' was not there three times but many times. Thank You Swami for Your early birthday gift, though I was still waiting for a gift from my Shirdi Sai. He did not forget too as the next story shows.

The Apple Story (2 October)

I went to the Shirdi Temple at Strathfield. We were given prasad and udhi and I helped myself to a rose lying at His Divine Lotus Feet. I stayed merely for a minute as I had to rush back to work and had a taxi waiting. The traffic was endless and I did not have enough money to pay the taxi. The bill came to about $35. I had only $25. I was embarrassed and scared at the same time, but God was always with me. I explained to the taxi driver that I had not enough money. He said, 'Pay me what You want'. I gave him $20 and kept $5 for lunch. At Newtown on alighting from the taxi, I noticed this lovely tall elderly distinguished gentleman with a sparkle in his eye. He smiled at me and I smiled back, just knowing it was my Shirdi Sai. I stopped at 'Taste' to buy some food for lunch, though I could not afford the dessert. While waiting for my change, a young waiter came up to me, very friendly and asked how I was and then proceeded to give me an apple. I remembered the apple I received at the Shirdi temple a year ago. Shirdi was once again with me for which I was grateful. It was as if He was confirming, 'I let you off the hook with the taxi fare, you saw me walk by and now I have even given you dessert'. Yes, I see God often. He is not only in my heart and soul, but everywhere with me. Coming home after work I was trying to remember Shiva's Abode. I said to Sai, 'Baba, what is the name? I know it starts with a K but I can't remember'. 'Kailash', He answered immediately. *Sai Ram.*

Darshan (4 October)
It was a very hurried and busy day since I was having fourteen people for lunch tomorrow. I also extended the invitation to the whole puja room. I hoped they would come in all their finery. Before rushing to the shops, I closed my eyes and got the most visual and peaceful vision of Shirdi Sai. I saw Lisa and me at His beautiful Lotus Feet. I said, '*Baba, apka haat humko do*'. I may have worded it incorrectly as I do not remember Hindi very well any more but meant to say, 'Baba please lay Your hand on us'. He replied, '*Thairo*/Wait'. He then came up to Lisa and me, placed His beautiful Hands on our heads and blessed us. This was while I was reciting the Gayatri mantra. I was very humbled and felt thankful. I opened my eyes to see His face in the pink portrait had started to give darshan. It was indescribable and stunningly beautiful. The face changed, the eyes rolled and it was no more a picture but flesh with tiger-like eyes. I felt extremely blessed. I finished reading the *Sai Satcharita.*

Vijayadashami/Mahasamadhi (5 October)
Though Shirdi Sai had left His mortal coil but to many He has never left, ever living-bones, flesh and all, and is very much in our midst. At bhajans today, I saw a flower fall at Swami's Lotus feet. Sairah gave me a box of chocolates for my birthday. A very happy birthday indeed. And God made His presence felt with His present in His

unusual way. A few days ago prior to this lunch, I was complaining to Shirdi as always 'Nobody has ever given me red long-stem roses' and gave this sentence not much thought after my whining. An old family friend and his mother who attended my birthday lunch today, surprised me with the most beautiful bunches of long-stemmed red and yellow roses. They were the bearers of the roses, but the doer who knows all and does all, my Shirdi Sai, sent them not one but two bunches. No thanks will ever be enough, one cannot give back to God what is His. Then to make His Presence even more subtle, Jeff (my brother) brought into the house a snake (Shiva), and everybody felt a bit scared and uncomfortable. So did I, but for some reason I got the courage to actually touch the snake. Shirdi Sai has for ever been with me, and I pray for Him to be with me even after life. Thank You for such a happy day.

Dream of Shirdi Sai (24 October)

In the dream Henry and I were in a Shirdi Masjid. There was a pujari praying and statues of Shirdi everywhere. Then I came across an empty space where a statue must have once stood and I asked the pujari what had happened to it. He answered, 'Sometimes He (Shirdi Sai) comes in here and takes what He likes'. I was very happy, I knew what the pujari meant. I gave dakshina. While he was holding it in his hand, two bullies entered the masjid and wanted the money, but the pujari would not give it to them. Then a boy entered, grabbed a small statue of Shirdi Sai and ran off. All went off in pursuit of the thief and caught him. The pujari gave me a picture and I think a small statue of Shirdi Sai. I was very happy. Henry and I then got into a helicopter and as we were quite high in the air I could see ahead of us a big black and white picture of Shirdi Sai staring straight at us. I got so excited and made Henry look too. What a beautiful dream!

The Whirling Dervishes (25 October)

I saw the show at the Opera House (The Whirling Dervishes—Sufi's) with Sharon and Gary. I loved the call of the Imam, in one part of the show, but not too much the Turkish country music, which I felt was too monotonous. After enjoying a lovely weekend with the Newells and Mum today, lunching at Chinatown and seeing the movie 'Calendar Girls', I wanted to get home before the storm hit. The sky was black as we approached Glenfield, the lightening and thunder was ferocious, and I was at my wits end with fear. Another four stations and we had to get off at Leumeah. We had no umbrellas and the storm was raging. I closed my eyes and prayed telling Shirdi Sai to please calm the storm, like He did for all His devotees in the *Sai Satcharita* so that they could go home safely. As we were approaching Minto it was still pouring and storming fiercely. The next stop was Leumeah. We pulled into Leumeah station and got off the train. It was still raining but by the time we got down the station steps, the rain suddenly stopped, the sky lightened, the black clouds rolled away, and we got home safely.

November

Darshan—Seeing God (11 November)

I had asked Shirdi Sai to hold my hand today (these thoughts and words come into my heart at random, whenever and wherever I am—my way of communicating with my Baba).

Walking towards the lifts at work, at about 11.00 a.m., I saw this very old, thin, frail but beautiful lady asking directions from a worker in the hospital. The worker was directing the old lady, but she still looked confused. I then asked her where she wanted to go, she stated 'to have a mammogram'. She was in the wrong building. I then proceeded to give her directions as to where Breast Screening was done. She then looked straight into my eyes, held my hands tightly and said I was very kind and thanked me. I then burst into tears, I was looking at my Shirdi Sai. He had held my hands as requested, in the form of a very old lady.

The Baba's Darshan (14 November)

It was a long, hot but very beautiful day. As usual I was rushing to see the cardiac specialist in Liverpool. In the corridor I saw a young lad with the biggest blue eyes staring at me. Shirdi Sai, I chuckled. After a long wait at the surgery (one hour waiting, though the specialist saw me for five minutes only, saburi), I rushed to catch a train home. I looked up at the beautiful blue sky to see Swami's jet steaming by. The Babas were with me during the consultation. I was very happy, not with the doctor though since we had to wait for hours and he had seen us only for minutes. I had decided not to continue with this specialist, who does not give much time to his patients.

Beautiful Darshan (22 November)

God is omnipresent and kind enough to show Himself when one longs to see Him. While making the fruit cake for Swami's birthday tomorrow I measured the flour wrongly. Thankfully, Shirdi brought my attention to the flour and I was corrected it. Then, after putting the cake in the oven, I realised that I had forgotten to add the vanilla and almond essences. I got more upset at my stupidity and poured the essences over the top while the cake had just started to bake. It looked okay, though I didn't know what it would taste like. I was very upset with my forgetfulness.

And the Rain Stopped (27 November)

Foolishly or forgetfully I did not take the umbrella, even though I could see the dark clouds hanging overhead. So I decided to continue on to Central Station instead of getting off at Redfern with no umbrella. Thankfully I saw one of my acquaintance waiting on the platform. As it was pouring he offered to share his umbrella with me. When we got off at McDonald town, there was no rain. It stayed clear till we reached work and then it started to pour again. What a loving and kind God, once again He stopped the rain and got us to work dry.

December

Trip–Away We Go to the Abode of Highest Peace—Puttaparthi (27 December)

I met a young man on the plane. We chatted about various things. He was on his way to Bangalore. Most of my conversation was about Shirdi Sai. He suddenly touched my feet and gave me Rs100 to put in the dakshina box. I asked him who his Guru was. He pulled out a picture from his wallet, Shirdi Sai. Oh, I felt such joy at seeing my Baba.

At Bangalore the hired car was not there. I was sitting alone at the airport, in the middle of the afternoon, tired and annoyed at all the hawkers staring from outside the airport. Ramdas, the young man, then appeared and said he was also waiting for his lift. As I spoke of my dilemma, he rang the car company in Parthy about the car since I could not speak the language. The car arrived two hours later, but thank God, it arrived.

28 December
I went late for darshan and found no cushion. There were new stone benches on the wall which meant no more sitting against the wall. I did seva after breakfast and was placed to serve the men in the canteen.

Om Shri Ganeshaya Namaha (30 December)
The dogs howled all night along with the donkeys braying. Not much sleep. I went early for darshan and presented my letter (I could not sit on the floor due to my arthritic knees) to the lady who was in charge of the Seva Dals. She told me to sit on the chair and she would give my letter to the lady in charge of seating in the hall, but I got nowhere. Then I decided to stand across from Swami's Abode, under the tree. Swami gave darshan from His car again, though brief, but it was worth seeing. I bought a rose for Ganesha and Shirdi.

My Thanks (31 December)
I thank You Shirdi Sai, Sathya Sai, Jesus, Mary and all for the year that is almost over.
Thank You for keeping the family and friends safe and in good health.
Thank You for Your never-ending Grace bestowed on me.
Thank You for Your saburi (patience), hearing my endless complaints to Thee.
Thank You my Shirdi Sai for being my Everything.
Thank You Swami for just being, please continue to be.
Thank You Jesus for Your sweetness, Thank You Holy Mother for taking care of Lisa.
Thanks to God and His Team.

2004

January

Beautiful Darshan/Lovely Leela—God Bless/Happy 2004 to All

I was woken up on the first day of 2004 by a bhajan group doing the rounds on the street. It was a very lovely way to start the New Year as such. This was an absolutely blissful darshan. I was thankful, and very humbled and grateful for receiving the magnificent darshan of Swami inside the Hall. After breakfast, I went to the garden to wish my Shirdi Sai a happy 2004. There was an Indian lady sitting at His feet. I was about to serve Him breakfast. I could not monopolise Him for He belongs to all. I greeted her and we started to chat about Him. She sounded like my clone. We did all the same things for and with Him. She had laid an ice cream at Shirdi Sai's feet. She opened a second one, put a bit on Baba's lips, took a mouthful and gave me the rest. Her name was Mira. Our thoughts and our hearts were so much alike. On the way back to Sai Sadan, I saw the frail, beautiful calm sweet man who reminded me of my Shirdi Sai. My heart told me it was Him in disguise. He slept on the road outside the hotel I stayed at, and I felt so close to him, he just reminded me of Shirdi Sai.

He Is with Me (2 January)

Swami came late. That was fine. He deserved rest after His busy day, the day before. My heart confirmed that the frail old man was surely my Shirdi Sai in human form. I say this with confidence as in the morning that day, before I had left the hotel for darshan I had requested Shirdi Sai, 'If I see the old man smoking a chillum today, I will know it is You'. I saw the old man smoking a chillum. I had a beautiful darshan of Swami on the morning of 3 January.

At the Ashram I got beautiful and long darshan of Swami. He very sweetly came 'hobbling' out of His home. I stood before the car. Facing us He stood before us for a minute. I was very happy. Swami played one of His tricks on me this morning. Our darshan was just about to end and all male Seva Dals and police were being drilled into forming a queue just behind where we were standing, outside of the hall. I was happy to think that 'Swami was going to pass this way'. The Seva Dal and police all stood to attention. After about half an hour, they were recalled. Swami decided to take a different route!

Beautiful Darshan (4 January)

Swami came out of His home. He did not go straight into the car. Swami just stood there in full view of us for quite a while giving us very beautiful darshan. I got so excited and happy that I waved. Swami just stared straight at me. Swami showered His loving grace and loving look on me.

5 January

I awoke late. I missed darshan, did no seva, simply because I was feeling lazy. However, I attended Sara Pavan's talk on modern day medicine. It was interesting, informative, funny and down to earth. We believed so much in the manuals of man forgetting the manuals of God. The mind dictates and we listen. When surrendering completely do not cling waiting for a result and hope for the same. Swami had endowed me with a few grains of wisdom. He mentioned that there have to be doctors, but this heart, mind, body, soul and being belong to God. He who created me, gave me life and breath, will take through it too.

Grace and Bliss (6 January)

Swami came out quite late today, around 7.30 a.m. I asked Swami prior to His darshan, to wave or put His hand up. Swami was very compassionate and obliging. He came out, stood a minute before entering the car, and gesticulated with His Divine Hand. It was close to 8.00 a.m., the Vedas were being chanted, I was close to fainting with hunger and so I decided to walk to the Western canteen. No one was there as darshan was still on in the Hall. I walked towards the north, heard a Seva Dal saying that Swami was going to drive past soon after darshan. At first, I thought this was another trick of Swami on my eavesdropping. But I noticed more and more Seva Dals forming queues. So I stood too and there He was. Swami drove past in His car right by me, I had the biggest grin on my face. Swami waved His hands and had I been quick enough, I could have touched the Divine hands in the car. I felt that Swami would return via the same route, so I ran across and yes, Swami came back. I shouted Swami gleefully, He looked straight into my eyes, smiled, waved His hands. It was so blissful I cried.

I did not go to darshan this morning, even though we were dressed for it. It was raining. After breakfast, I did some seva in the kitchen, helping to wipe dishes, and then went to attend the bhajans. The rains had stopped. I attended a lecture by Robert and Rita Bruce, a very beautiful and spiritual couple. I truly believed in practicality, spirituality and common sense with a touch of wisdom combined with God's Will and complete surrender to Him. We were very blessed to have Swami there and we should have given the opportunity and take every advantage of it. We may be His instruments but we have to make an effort, 'have a go' and leave the results to Him or whomsoever one believes in.

Amazing Grace (8 January)

I was awoken by the troupe of bhajan singers again going by on the street. What a wonderful start to the day, which was glorious. I got great darshan from Swami, then another darshan of Swami going past in the car. He was smiling and waving His beautiful hands. Before the start of bhajans, Swami came back right past again with a cavalcade of motor cyclists preceding Him in a very 'swish' white car. The afternoon darshan started late. I was very blessed to have had five glorious darshans of Swami today. After darshan I went to Anantapur with the 'bodyguards (the manager and the boy)' from the hotel where I stayed. There were a line of temples and it was crowded and hot. The Shirdi Temple was the last at the top of the hill, to get to but I was determined to go in even though it was almost ready to close for lunch. I had to go through throngs of people, cars, bikes. I bought His favourite fruit guavas/bananas as offering. The line was long and they were about to close the gates. My heart sank. I wanted to get near enough to the murti, even if it were for a second. He looked as splendid as ever. The pujari took the fruit, blessed the same, and got me up close and personal to the murti. He gave me a rose and to my utter disbelief, the pujari invited me to his room located next to the temple. I was hesitant but I realised it was my Shirdi Sai's invitation via the pujari, so I went along with the boy as my ever constant bodyguard. It was a little room, humble and cosy. The pujari gave the boy some money and told him to buy two laddoos for me. I was taken aback, I had always been asking the Babas to give me laddoos. He then asked me to sit on a chair, and started to converse with me in Hindi. I responded back in Hindi and even though I had not spoken the language in thirty-five years, I spoke quite fluently. The pujari asked me how I spoke so well, to which I had no answer. We then spoke of Baba and then the pujari said that he was actually from Shirdi, and was sent here to oversee the temple. After the laddoos, the pujari then bought me a ring (from my Shirdi Sai of course) with Shirdi Sai written in silver on it and a beautiful black and white picture of Him. There was a lady standing near to me. She had very beautiful eyes and kept staring at me (I knew it was Him). He always showed Himself to me with those eyes. It was a lovely day. At afternoon darshan back in the Ashram, tears welled in my eyes, as the quiet lady who stands beside me every day held my hand with such sweetness and sincerity. She did this every day, morning and afternoon, before Swami came out. She stood behind me under the tree. We had darshan of Swami. After the bhajans she held my hand for a minute, and then disappeared. No words were ever spoken between the two of us.

9 January

It was good to have had Swami's car darshan four times this morning. I chased the car everywhere and got the darshan. I went looking for a picture of Ayappa for a friend in Australia who was a devotee. I had no luck. The boy took me to the temple complex across from the hotel. There was a small shrine of Ayappa there. The pujari there called me and kindly gave me the only picture of Ayappa he had in the temple, so kind of him.

10 January

I had darshan again. I loved scrambling from one end of the Nilayam to the other. Swami was keeping me fit. We all chased Swami's car. Swami very kindly did look my way and waved His hands. I was very humbled and grateful.

I was disappointed at not having Swami's darshan for the last time, as I would be leaving for Goa on the same day. It was also Sports day, and Swami was going straight to the stadium. On waking up, I asked Swami, 'I don't like to leave without Your darshan, it is not comforting, please let me see You once before I leave'. I went to the Nilayam to get some water for the journey ahead and to also say farewell to Ganesha, and there He was, Swami, in the car on the way to the stadium. Once again I got a wonderful view, and a wonderful darshan. I was very happy. Next, prior to arriving at the Shirdi Temple on the way to Bangalore, the driver in the car gave me a packet of vibhuti, also narrating the story behind it that the vibhuti had materialised from a picture at the Super Speciality Hospital in Bangalore. It was apparently only accessible to the doctors there. One of the doctors gave three packets to this driver when he was being driven to Parthy. The driver in turn very kindly shared a packet with me. Such bountiful grace! I arrived at the hotel in Bangalore. I opened the telephone directory, and the first picture I saw was one of Swami.

Sankranti—Utter Grace (14 January)

I whispered to Swami that I was missing His darshan tremendously. I opened the newspapers, there He was along with the Infant Jesus and St. Jude and I was in bliss supreme. Before leaving the hotel for Goa, I wanted so much to have darshan of Lord Ganesha. On entering the car there were eleven pictures stuck everywhere of Ganapati! I began to sing in joy, You take all the obstacles away – Lord Gananatha. We were informed by a kindly Goan gentleman on the plane where to get a taxi etc., in Goa, as this was our first trip and we did not know a thing about Goa. On getting to the Taxi Office at Goa Airport, I nearly fell over. There were pictures of my Shirdi Sai everywhere. I was ecstatic. In the taxi too, He was there. I had earlier said to Shirdi Sai, 'I have not seen You today in some form. I know that You are travelling along with me. I saw Swami, Ganesha, Jesus, and all and what about You?' The driver of the taxi was also a devotee. Shirdi Sai temples were coming up everywhere in Goa as He was getting more and more popular. I loved Goa, even more so now, that He was everywhere even in Goa.

Darshan and Fun in Goa (15 January)

I woke up early and was happy to see a big 'Om' flag just across a balcony while looking out of the window. It was the balcony of an art gallery. At 9.30 a.m. the bus arrived which I boarderd to go on a tour in Goa. I went to the Bom Jesus Cathedral where the body of St. Francis Xavier lay. Goa is very exotic and quaint at the same time. The greenery is vast and soothes the eye. After lunch I hurriedly tried to pay and run to the bus as there was a squabble between a European man and the hotel manager where we stopped for lunch. They were almost coming to blows, I was a bit afraid. I looked up from my meal to make a hasty exit and there on the wall was my Shirdi Sai in picture. I felt safe. It was the last stop on the beach, and I was just about to board the bus to come home, when I heard the sound of a helicopter. I looked up and there was Swami (the jet steam) and the copter. Also I got the darshan of beautiful pictures of our Lady and Jesus. It had been a blessed day indeed.

The Guide (16 January)

What an exciting morning it had been. Satish (the guide) was very informative about Goa, and the architecture, the colours of the old buildings were magnificent. The Goan families welcomed us off the street into their homes. They were kind and warm hearted. I loved them. I got darshan of my Baba. He was certainly everywhere in Goa. My heart stopped and smiled silently whenever I saw another picture of Him. I visited my Baba's temple in Panjim. He looked resplendent with a twinkle in His eye. The guide took a picture of us. I could never express clearly the joy at seeing my Shirdi Sai.

More Grace Was to Come (17 January)

In my dream I watched a cart go by with a murti of my Shirdi Sai. I beamed and waved. The dream ended. I went to another big temple (new) of Shirdi Sai in Goa. It was very beautiful, the murti being very lifelike. I garlanded my beloved Baba and left the place with a lot of peace.

Last Day in Goa (18 January)

At the airport, a lady tapped me on the shoulder and asked, 'Are you going to see Swami? I noticed your ring'. I informed her that I had already seen Swami in Parthy and had seen a great deal of Shirdi Sai in Goa. At Bangalore I was given a rose, and saw a beautiful picture of Swami. I felt like Swami was saying: 'Come back'. I wish I could Swami, but I had to go back to Sydney and back to work. On the plane sitting near me was a very young Indian girl. We started to chit-chat and she had just been to Shirdi and Parthy and told me that Swami gave her a statue of Goddess Lakshmi. Well, perhaps I should go back to Parthy, too late now, can't halt the plane. Farewell my beloved India, until the next time, soon I hope.

The Hand (23 January)

While in Parthy at darshan in the morning and afternoon, a serene Indian lady would stand behind me every day and pray very reverentially when Swami entered and exited. She was always the last to move and only did so after Swami's door was closed. After that she used to hold my hand for a minute, looking into my eyes and moved on. I often wondered about this 'sweet gesture of hers'. Not only was she holding my hand ever so gently but was also looking at me directly into my eyes. I felt as if Shirdi Sai was holding my hands.

The Storm (24 January)

I had a short darshan of Swami's Divine Lotus Feet and Shirdi Sai's eyes. After having lunch with Mum and Lisa, we were to return home having to travel a long journey back home. Dark threatening clouds were looming above us and I was not too happy becoming anxious of being caught up in a terrible storm while returning home. I prayed to the calmer of the storms—Shirdi Sai to take it away. Once again, my kind, Baba let the sun come through out of all that black sky. The wind stopped howling, the rain stopped, and we got home safe and dry. I opened the front door, as I reached home, the storm started right away.

What can I say to such a sweet compassionate Deva, who knows my every fear, and always makes them disappear for me. Such Grace. Much thanks.

Miracles (27 January)

I had a dream at 3.30 a.m. I saw Mum pointing to the sky. I looked up to see a very black cloud, which then turned to light and we watched Our Lady there. I got excited, looked up again to see the dark cloud again, but Our Beautiful Holy Mother was there. My dream ended. I think Our Lady was telling us that She was always with us too. Thank You Holy Mother. We love You. Apprehensive about going back to work after such a long, lovely holiday, I asked the Babas to keep me calm. There was the jet steam. Swami was with me.

I got to work to find I was promoted, from a grade 3 to a 5, my humble thanks to You.

Om Shri Ganeshaya Namaha. I was missing India much already.

February

Dream (7 February)

In my dream I was giving oil and vibhuti to a lady who appeared ill. Then I saw two female pujaris blessing me, doing aartis and putting vibhuti twice on my forehead. The dream ended here. I could now recall asking the Babas for Their blessings before I fell off to sleep tonight. Thank You Babas.

Valentine's Day (14 February)

This year I never pestered Shirdi Sai for roses or anything, but He never forgot Valentine's Day as He played my most favourite piece of music, that only He knew I loved so very much, from the time I was a little girl. 'Moonglow', the original version, which was very rarely heard these days. I realised it was the Valentine leela that He never failed to send me on this day.

Divine Intervention (17 February)

Lisa rang from Ireland to say that her camera, (which she uses for work) was stolen, so was her visa card and asked me to look for the camera receipt, which was kept in a box in the garage, and to post it to her for an insurance claim. There were about twenty-seven boxes of hers in the garage and I was in a tizz as to which one to open up first, or perhaps I would have to open them all up to find that elusive receipt. Before entering the garage I prayed, 'Please Baba help me to find the receipt quickly. It would be too tiring to have to go through all those boxes'. The garage was also housing a friend's car while they were in Parthy, and there was no room to move, so I would have to hurdle over boxes and I did not want to set the car alarm off. With much hesitance and bated breath, I opened the garage door. The boxes were stacked on either side of the car as well as at the back. I immediately felt like closing the garage door again, but this had to be done. I inched my way to the back, I noticed boxes with the words Books/Papers marked on them. There were about eight of these, which one to open first? The one closest to me was opened. There was a folder in which Lisa said she kept all her receipts, while I was hopeful and praying even quicker than opening the boxes, I looked under 'C'. It was there, the camera receipt! Thank You Babas.

Mahashivaratri (18 February)

I always got excited on Mahashivaratri every year, as stated earlier, vowing to repeat *Om Namah Shivaya* (started on 9 February) and to complete on the same day for 18,000 times. I prayed to Shiva to send me a signal when I had made the chantings the number of times I had vowed I went to the library to borrow some books. The first book I looked at was *Shiva*. It was the first acknowledgement from Shiva. I went home to find that *Sanathana Sarathi* had arrived (it usually arrives at the end of each month), which was the second sign from Shiva. *Om Namah Shivaya*.

March

Vibhuti (2 March)

I had been reading the book *A Blind Man Meets Sai Baba on the Road to Puttaparthi* by Luigi A. Sacco. I loved his humour, his frankness, and his openness. Many times on opening a chapter of this book I used to get a very strong smell of vibhuti bursting forth. Beautiful leela!

Dream (4 March)

It was quite a long and colourful dream. I could hear Lord Ganesha's name being repeated by a little girl who said she liked the sound of it and I was repeating the same. Next, while gazing at the sky, I saw Swami standing on a large grey cloud, wearing a grey robe with His arms outstretched to me. I floated up towards Swami, very excited. Then I saw myself at a table wearing an orange robe, surrounded by people with all types of beautiful cakes, (in real life I love baking cakes). I noticed a friend standing by with a cherry cake and I mentioned Swami to her. My dream came to an end.

Darshan (14 March)

I watched a video called 'Stigmata'. I was very touched on seeing Padre Pio and St. Francis of Assisi, both stigmatists. I have always felt very close to them and now more so to Papa Pio. He looked so much like my Shirdi Sai. At the moment of writing this, there is a divine fragrance enveloping this room. At afternoon prayer, I got a beautiful darshan of Shirdi Sai. He kept opening and closing His serene and very beautiful eyes, ever so gently. Then I saw His silhouette very clearly, and the white light.

The Rainbow (18 March)

I have urged the Babas to please show me a rainbow before 22 March, which would indicate me to begin my work on the book. On the way to work today, the sky was clear and blue but there was a rainbow. My prayer had been answered.

Prayer Answered (22 March)

Earlier this evening I was trying, with no success, to get the name of Mother Theresa's homes in Calcutta. So I prayed for help in finding the name. I received ten e-mails, one from a Sai devotee in India stating how he helped a dying sick beggar by taking her to 'The Little Sisters of the Poor' (Mother Theresa's group), where she could leave her mortal coil in dignity.

Travel Sign (26 March)

On leaving Parthy earlier this year, I had boldly asked the Babas if I could return again to Parthy and Shirdi, with the Grace of God. While the confirmation from the Babas were positive at the time of making the request, I pestered the Babas, yet again, if I could start making plans for Parthy and Shirdi. One more sign was necessary to go ahead with the bookings. I received a fax from a colleague at work, which was three pages long, telling us about her trip around the world particularly of India. Here was my sign from the Babas to go ahead with the plans for the journey to Shirdi and Parthy.

April

4 April

At bhajans this morning, while Savita's mother was singing, a huge rose fell from Swami's picture followed soon by a heavy downpour or rain. It was startling to say the least as we were suffering a severe drought. Thank You beloved Swami.

Darshan (17 April)

I had a very awesome darshan of Shirdi Sai from the pink picture. For some reason, this colour had been occurring to me for most of this week. His loving and kindly eyes gently moved, His face beckoned and it became so lifelike, that it seemed as if one would feel flesh had one touched His face. With God's Grace I wished my journey be even more inward bound, for He stays in my heart.

May

Amazing Grace (3 May)

I visited the oncologist for a throat check-up. Funnily enough, I was not nervous at all but was looking forward to meet the doctor, a very kindly man. The jet steam was flying high against a beautiful sky. Swami was with me going to the hospital. I met the doctor, whom I have not seen for seven years. He recognised me immediately and attended me with such care and time which was very unlike a busy doctor like him. Thank You Shirdi Sai for ever being with me. The examination results were good—I had no saliva but my throat was fine.

Beautiful Grace (8 May)

In my dream I saw myself in a room with my grandmother, mother and an Indian couple. The room was filled with pictures of Shirdi Sai on the walls. As usual, I was very excited, trying to explain to my grandmother (who in reality has left her mortal coil) that 'That Was My Shirdi Sai'. The Indian lady then started to tell me how much she too loved Shirdi Sai and how He had answered Her prayers so quickly. My dream ended. I awoke very happy having seen my Shirdi Sai in a dream. At morning aarti, there were those godly eyes, beckoning, so softly, so gently. I had a chit-chat with Him, may His Will be always done for me. Next I smelled a rather aromatic fragrance, but could not decipher the same. Was it camphor, or chandan or some other divine fragrance? *Om Sai Shri Sai Jai Jai Sai.*

Sweet Sai Leela (26 May)

I worked so hard today that by the time it was 4 p.m., I was thoroughly exhausted and was dreading the long trudge back home. It used to take me four trains and three hours a day to travel to and from work every day. I whispered to Baba on the train home, 'I am not looking forward to the long cold walk home in the dark, could you *fly* me home?' I got off the train, a man (my kind neighbour) came up to me and said, 'Wait a minute Lorraine, I will just get a loaf of bread and drop you home'. My prayer was answered almost immediately.

Those who believe and do the right: Joy is for them and bliss their journey's end (Holy Koran).

June

The Star (27 June)

As I wake up every morning, the first thing I do is to go to the window and watch the brightest star in the sky—my Shirdi Sai, then there is Swami and Jesus. After my prayer to all these heavenly beings, I start the day. Today the Morning Star was the biggest I have ever witnessed, big, bright and beautiful. I stared open-mouthed. It was like really looking straight at God.

Leelas (30 June)

First thought on waking this morning was 'God please let me experience You today'. He did.

(a) A jet steam was flying against a beautiful blue sky (Swami).

(b) I saw a tall, elegant and beautifully garbed Muslim man in Newtown, wearing a kafni surrounded by his children. The only thing missing was the scarf (Shirdi Sai).

(c) The word 'Travel', once again confirming the Babas' permission for our trip to India, on a billboard.

(d) An unfamiliar advertisement on TV for a travel agent: 'The Guru Says—Travel'.

I often intoned the Babas 'May I experience Thee', I guess I just knew the signs of the Babas. No ego here, just a mere truth. On asking for signs, when sent, it is recognised instantly.

July

Guru Poornima (2 July)

The Morning Star shone bright. I asked the Baba if repeated the *Om Sai Shri Sai, Jai Jai,* 18,000 times as promised for Guru Poornima, the first five clustered numbers would be His answer to me. There was a large billboard with a new poster on it with the numbers 19,890. Thank You Baba, I was happy with going above the numbers stated. There was amazing fragrance of vibhuti after this as a further confirmation. May I take this opportunity to say Thank You to Shirdi Sai, Sathya Sai, Jesus Sai and all the sweet and sacred Gurus of this universe. May the Guru be praised. Divinely the figures add to nine.

Whosoever searches for joy eternal, let him seek that in All pervading naam (quote from the holy book of the Sikhs).

Nausea/Dream (6 July)

I have been feeling unwell and nauseous for the last ten days or more, perhaps the diet was wrong or I was not eating enough. I even had a dream where I was lying in a surgery. The surgeon looked like Shirdi Sai and was about to perform abdominal surgery on me and he kept saying in the operating theatre, 'the food eaten was wrong'. My dream ended here. After this dream I thought it was the lack of food that was making me feel so ill. I kept praying and asking, 'Baba, why am I feeling so ill, I am not vomiting, no diarrhoea, just nausea, which is not going away. Please tell me what is wrong'. Please note here dear reader, whenever I feel ill, I either take vibhuti or speak to the Babas instead, until I feel well again. This however was now going into weeks, and I was still feeling nauseous. That morning after praying and asking again I went to get the butter out of the fridge, and something made me look at its manufacturing date. It was three weeks' old. Baba told me in the dream about the food being wrong and actually showed me the date. Baba also knew how I disliked vomiting. I also *had* to go to work in spite of feeling so poorly. He took me through all of this in His inimitable way.

August

20 August

What a beautiful day it was, the sky was blue, sun was shining. I was travelling into the City to visit the Shirdi Temple at Strathfield. The temple doors were closed but I got beautiful darshan of my Baba through the keyhole. On our way back, we stopped at the Indian shops in Liverpool. Shirdi Sai has a favourite pickle (sweet brinjal—i.e., bharit), but it is very difficult to buy. It is never in stock and have been now been searching for the same for the last two years. Once again, I went through the line of pickles, and there was a dusty bottle at the back.

Darshan (21 August)

Mum and I went to Chinatown for lunch, after which we stopped at the Peter Julian Church for a visit. The beautiful Host was exposed and out of respect, love and remembrance, I should have knelt before the Sacred Heart of Jesus' body, but my ego got in the way so also my worn out knees got in the way and I did not kneel. For those who are not familiar with the exposition of the Host, this is a brief summary. In some churches the Host (or body of Christ) is exposed to all and one is usually meant to kneel before the Host in reverence. Coming home in the train, I began to feel very ill. My head was spinning (no I did not drink any wine, just ate), the stomach bloated, the immune system was breaking down. I got home feeling wretched. At prayer, I thanked Shirdi Sai for reminding me of the ego by allowing me to feel so ill. He may spoil me but when I deserve to be 'told off' for doing the wrong thing, He does that too. I then looked at the picture of the Sacred Heart in the altar room, asked Jesus for His forgiveness, and told Him that I loved Him very much, and to forgive my bad behaviour ending with the words 'God forgive and come to me'. The most beautiful darshan in the form of the white light began emanating from the picture of the Sacred Heart of Jesus and only from this picture. It lasted for about five minutes and it was very calm, soothing and beautiful. The light shone from Jesus' Face and His Heart. Then the coloured pictured turned into black and white and then back to the Divine Light on the coloured picture. I felt very forgiven, very blessed and very thankful. Lord, remind me for ever to do that which is right by all, especially God.

Laughter and Tears (26 August)

In my dream I saw a large open space filled with miniscule statues of Shirdi Sai everywhere, and with people doing puja. I beckoned to the sister to hurry up as we had to find a very large statue of Shirdi Sai, with me being very excited (what's new). The dream ended here.

I was standing in a queue at the bank, a lady in front of me was wearing a T-shirt reading 'BA BA BA BA – And That's The End of It'. I was waiting for a reply from the Babas. Tears—a tooth had fallen out—and once again I had to make a dental visit.

I was walking back to my home when I saw the jet steam. I was consoled by Swami.

A Family Tragedy (31 August)

I was just about to leave for work at 6.30 a.m. this morning, when the phone rang. Nobody used to ring at this hour or the day, my heart sank. It was my sister with some sad news. Our beloved niece Sharon, who lived in Western Australia, had been killed instantly by a truck. She was only twenty-nine years old.

September

Perth, Western Australia (7 September)

The funeral of our beloved child Sharon. She was a child of God, a child of the universe. She was His creation and into His arms she had returned. We love you darling Sharon, may you rest in His arms.

11 September

I felt a deep sorrow in my heart. My thoughts were with Dixie (Sharon's mother and her sister Kelly and our family too). God help us all to get through this. At morning prayer today, I poured out my sorrowed heart. I got a brief darshan from Swami from the picture with the flower behind and then I received much darshan from the pink picture of Shirdi Sai (Sharon's favourite colour, her whole beautiful funeral was pink based). Shirdi Sai's face turned to flesh, it made me comforted and peaceful. I knew that there would be many hours of need and sorrow for a while, but I knew He is ever watching. Please take care of Dixie and Kelly and the rest of our sorrowed family.

Car Accident (17 September)

I was invited to Sue and Dan's house for dinner to discuss their first visit to Shirdi. Their daughter dropped me home later and on the way back we had a car accident. Thankfully we escaped injury, but we were in shock. I realised later that this was a jolt to me, as her parents were off to Shirdi in a week and I completely forgot to send some prasad or dakshina for my Shirdi Sai.

Forgetfulness Again (18 September)

I begged Lord Ganesha to forgive me for my forgetfulness. I did not remember Ganesh Chaturthi today. Therefore, I failed to repeat *Om Shri Ganapati Namaha*. I asked His forgiveness and requested darshan (even though I was not deserving of the same after forgetting Ganesha). On the way home from the City, I saw a miniscule jet steam go by. Thank You dear Swami. All was forgiven.

The JP Miracle (24 September)

I was becoming a JP (Justice of the Peace) today. I got to the court in time and was asked to wait outside Court 6 until it was in session. There was a young man (he looked Indian) sitting next to me with the same JP letter that I had. My curiosity was aroused and I asked him if he was going to be sworn in as a JP too, to which he nodded his assent and introduced E as Victor, stating he was from Fiji. We started to chat almost immediately about Shirdi Sai. He noticed the ring with Shirdi Sai worn by me and that's how the conversation began (much to my joy and excitement of talking about Shirdi Sai I forgot my own nervousness on becoming a JP). He stated that he and his wife would be visiting Shirdi for the first time in December that year, and also mentioned his grandmother in Fiji being an ardent devotee of Shirdi Sai. He then stated he was a financial planner, I was even more astounded. For the last two years now I had been trying to find someone to help with the finances, particularly superannuation, but financial planners were either not interested in a paltry sum of money like mine or expected too much money as fees. It was like Victor and I were meant to meet regarding getting 'the money affairs' in order. Shirdi Sai knew how much I was concerned about this, and once again He, in His inimitable way, sent the right person at the right time. Saburi/Nishta. He always does everything for His devotees, at His own time, one just have to remember to be a little more patient.

The judge was a very noble man. After we were sworn in, he gave a speech as to how he became a JP in the same court room thirty years ago, how noble a position it was to be in, to help the community and congratulated us.

Darshan (25 September)

At morning aarti I was blessed with beautiful darshan from my pink Shirdi Sai picture. He was the Doer and knew exactly what was going on everywhere. Though I had to remind myself of this constantly, I poured out my heart to Him all the same about the bullies, one encounters every day. His beautiful eyes gave me such comfort, He does not have to speak. I understand His eyes. Then I got darshan from the picture of Jesus, The Divine Mercy. I had earlier asked for Divine Mercy and now received it from Jesus, too. It was very beautiful and soothing.

Practice simplicity in habits, simplicity of heart and simplicity of character (Quoted from Zarathushtra).

October

The Manuscript (10 October)

At morning prayer, I tearfully asked Baba/Swami if the title of the manuscript could be named *I Am Always With You*, and if this was an apt title, could I please have a sign. The manuscript was now being edited, pictures placed in position and was hopefully to be finished before we left for Shirdi/Parthy at the end of that year, with God's Grace. Baba's beautiful eyes at prayer (the pink picture of Shirdi Sai) closed very gently, a light came over them, then the eyes opened and closed and opened and closed. I felt like Baba had just answered my question about the title of the would-be book and my tears flowed in gratitude. Again later at prayer in the afternoon, Swami's face was covered by Light. My heart felt this was what the book should be named *I Am Always With You.* Thus shall it be if He Wills it to be.

Thy Will Will Be Done (17 October)

On the way to the Shirdi Temple in Strathfield, I got a panic attack, worrying about the crowds that would be at the temple and also at the approaching storm. I just wanted to be alone with my Sai, even in His temple. I had a chuckle on the train where a man boarded and set up an altar on his seat. He was wearing a broad ribbon with the words 'Holy Trinity' on it. He filled a vase with some paper flowers, placed a statue of Jesus, a rosary and began to say aloud, 'Jesus is travelling with us too', and how right he was. I loved it. At the temple at 9.00 a.m. I was astounded to see only two men inside. It was not crowded at all. One was dressing Baba's murti and the other was quietly reading the *Sai Satcharita*. Baba never failed to show me His kindness in so many ways. It was blissful to be alone with Him. I even got bold enough to venture up to the murti and to take a gardenia (He allowed me to, knowing this to be my favourite flower), off from His feet, and I wore it in my hair all day. Thank You my Beloved Everything, You are Everything to me. I left before the crowds started to pour in and I was so grateful to have a quiet moment in the temple with Him. He accommodated my simple wish to be alone with Him. At noon prayer at home, I apologised for having been scared. Baba returned the most kindest, humblest and sweetest darshan from the pink picture with His soft and loving eyes. *Om Sai Shri Sai Jai Jai Sai.*

Sit quiet, I will do the needful. I will take you to the end. Why are you anxious? so says Shirdi Sai.

True to His word – He always does, but the human that I am, I still worry (excerpts from *God Who Walked On Earth*: p. 57).

A Day of Miracles (23 October)

It was very early morning, around 5.00 a.m. when I had a dream. In my dream I saw all the ladies attending bhajans were talking with tears in their eyes. I could not understand what they were saying. Joy (from our bhajan group) then turned to me and whispered, 'They want to have a bhajan'. I replied, 'Why don't they have it in my house?'. My dream ended here.

Before going food shopping, at prayer I received a beautiful darshan from Shirdi Sai's eyes. His Eyes became alive and the darshan was awesome. Then I made a request before leaving: Baba, it would be nice to see Pushpa (a friend who worked with me in Liverpool hospital) at the mall. I have not seen her since her dear husband passed away a few months ago and she was still grieving. I finished shopping and was just about to hail a taxi when there she was Pushpa. I was able to pay my condolences. Words fail me with the kindness of Shirdi Sai. He is a miracle in itself.

Dusserah and Tamarind Stories (24 October)

Being Dusserah, I decided to make one of Baba's favourite dishes for Him, bharit. I must be insane, as I was no cook and could not cook any Indian dish. I had just finished reading the *Sai Satcharita* and it stated that He savoured bharit. It was not a good start, as I could not get tamarind while shopping yesterday and was getting concerned as this was one of the main ingredients in this dish. Besides my bigger concern was that I had promised Baba that I would make this dish for Him and I did not want to disappoint Him. After bhajans, I decided to catch a train to Liverpool where there were many Indian shops and I bought some tamarind there. I also bought an Indian paper which would tell us when the Deepavali Fair would be on and where. Then I became anxious to catch the train to Liverpool as a terrible storm was brewing and I was almost about to change my mind about going at all or even cooking the bharit. After bhajans, I asked kind Henry to drop me to the station to catch a train to Liverpool, he asked me why I was going to Liverpool and I said I needed some tamarind. 'We have plenty of delicious Fiji tamarind at home, I will give you some,' said he.

On the way to his car I overheard a couple talking about the Deepavali Fair, and quaintly mentioning the place, the date and the time. Baba saved me a trip to Liverpool in the storm, gave me delicious tamarind for his bharit through Henry and even indicated the dates for the Fair through the couple.

November

7 November

A rose fell at Swami's Divine Lotus Feet at bhajans this morning while Radha was singing. I felt very happy for Radha. He picked up the Divine blessed flower after bhajans. I was waiting to catch a train to the city after bhajans and were sitting at Minto station when an old world steam train (Thomas the Tank) went by, blowing its lovely whistle and we all waved at each other while the train went by. One rarely gets a glimpse of old steam trains any more, so it was delightful and unexpected to see this one (my Shirdi Sai enjoyed it too, I could feel the smile on His divine face).

A Day of Grace (18 November)

On waking up I requested Shirdi Sai to fill the day with His Grace, irrespective of the fact if I deserved it or not. I played some bhajans and I began to cry when '*Sai Bhajana Bina Shukha Santhi Nahi*' played and it reminded me of Swami always singing the same very sweetly in the Nilayam and also on CDs. Then I noticed the leaves in the pot in the lounge room starting to shake vigorously. The fan was not on, the doors were not opened and there was no wind. Were they dancing or crying too?

His Divine Will (19 November)

You must develop this attitude of merging with the Divine in all that you do. This attitude of dedication, of surrender to His Will. This is the best means of realising Him (excerpts from Swami's Religion of Love 2004 diary).

The manuscript was sent to Parthy about two months ago and was either lost, sent back to me by sea mail or God only knew what had happened to it. However, I have not heard anything back from The Book Trust in Prashanti to whom I had mailed the manuscript or part of it as it was still incomplete. I had a dream in early morning that the manuscript was posted back, therefore, in reality, I was anxious I had not received the same. At prayer I requested Baba/Swami thus 'We have five weeks left to travel to Shirdi/Parthy, if it be Thy Will, should we reprint the manuscript and take it to India with us? If there was a yes from You, please show me three jet steams today (Swami's yes sign to me) and let me add nineteen figures totalling nine (eighteen times – Shirdi Sai's yes sign to me). I would take these signs and assure that the book could be completed.

Within an hour of my request I saw three of the most awesome jet steams, in the most unlikely places, one actually merged with surya (sun) and it was like looking at God blessing me. Then not eighteen but almost thirty-eight numbers all the way to work added up to the figure nine (car number plates) and by God's Will and grace the last entry in this journal would be completed on Swami's 79th birthday (23 November 2004). The manuscript would be taken to Shirdi and Parthy as to whether it was to be printed and published as *Let Thy Will Be Done*.

After work, the sky was black and looked very threatening. I cowered and prayed to let it rain but not to be accompanied by a storm. At Leumeah station, it poured heavily, hailed but did not storm. I reached home soaked, opened the letterbox, saw a letter and tried to take it out when I found that there was a huge huntsman spider lying under the letter. I froze and dropped the letter and spider on the wet earth. Like storms, I was scared of spiders, especially this one, that looked more like a tarantula. After my initial shock I picked up the letter and ran to the front door, thanking Baba for first scaring me with the spider and then protecting me from it by not allowing it to jump onto my hand. Once again, He stopped the storm, even though the sky was black. He never allowed the spider to crawl up my hand, which it could have easily done. He was ever there and He ever cared for me. Many thanks to the Babas.

23 November

A very Happy Birthday to You Swami. I think I made my 18,000 time *Sai Ram* naam mantra, therefore requesting Swami: 'Swami, the first of any five figures we see today, will be the number of *Sai Rams* I have uttered this week for Your birthday'. The Billboard showed 18,002. I also saw the jet steam, another confirmation from sweet Swami that the number of *Sai Ram's* uttered by me was met. Happy Birthday again and many thanks to Swami.

December

And the Darshan Came Back (12 December)

And it happened again—the darshan from the pink picture. It was like a continuation from yesterday. Words could not describe the way His beautiful eyes moved. He spoke through the silence of His eyes. Thank You Baba.

We had a week left for Christmas. As there was much to be done, with the permission of Shirdi Sai, Sathya Sai and Jesus Sai too, we came to the conclusion of this simple book. My thanks will never be adequate to my Shirdi Sai, I can only humbly request that I may be worthy to earn His Divine Grace forever. I thank You Swami, love us ever, leave us never and to my dear Jesus, who came into my life and heart the day I was born, and is still there.

Many thanks to my dear family, friends and readers. Now you know how and why *He Is Always With Me*.

Epilogue

I recently met a gentleman who comes to Australia from India about every two years and does the Nadi reading. A friend of mine who sees and knows him and a lot of other people as well, took me to have my Nadi leaves done. Here are the excerpts of what the man (Senthik Kumar) said.

'This lady has a guru. The guru is the incarnation of Shiva. The incarnation of Shiva, Shirdi Ishwara. It is Shirdi Baba. He gives her darshan quite often. Shirdi Sai Baba has come to her house and lives with her. He gives darshan in the form of light and He comes in her photos. He lives with her in the house. Sometimes you have visions of Him, only you can see Him not anyone else. You have that kind of shakti. You have the shakti for speaking to Baba, communicating with Him.

You suffered in your younger days and mid life. At this stage you have fully come into spiritual life. You are living for Shirdi Sai Baba. Shirdi Sai Baba will do some miracles at your house. He will come quite often and bless you.

In your previous life's karma, you did good and bad deeds. You were born in Bharath, Maharashtra state in a place called Nasik into a Brahmin family as a boy. You were not interested in education. Your father tried to teach you Vedas, you were not interested. You went to a guru nearby. He was Shirdi Baba. You had a lot of spiritual involvement with Him and He was your Guru in your previous life too. He gave you disksha (I believe it means spiritual instructions) and you learned spiritual secrets from Him and a lot of spiritual information from your guru. Baba said to you, 'You came to me in your young age. You have a lot of spiritual knowledge. You have a lot to do in this life. Don't leave me and go. You have to stay with me and do a lot of service to poor people, orphans and sick people'.

But you as a young man, got interested in a beautiful young lady living near the Ashram. You left Baba half way through to have a family life. Because of the desire for a woman, you left the guru and guru was very upset. He thought of you as a perfect disciple. He thought that the disciple will come back and with this disciple, I will do a lot of good deeds. But you were interested in the lady and left your guru. You lived happily with the lady for a while. At fifty years you remembered your guru. You repented leaving the guru, left the family and wanted to help the guru. But you couldn't have the darshan of the guru. He said that in this life (past life) you cannot have me as your guru. You left the spiritual life for a woman and in your next life you will be born as a woman, when the guru will come back to you. You heard this in His voice—'When you realise that you get happiness only through spirituality, then I will return to you in your next life.'

Strangely enough Baba did come back into my life this time around when I turned fifty!